Iran: Time for a New Approach

*Report of an Independent Task Force
Sponsored by the
Council on Foreign Relations*

Zbigniew Brzezinski and Robert M. Gates,
Co-Chairs
Suzanne Maloney, Project Director

OCM 56725067

Founded in 1921, the Council on Foreign Relations is an independent, national membership organization and a nonpartisan center for scholars dedicated to producing and disseminating ideas so that individual and corporate members, as well as policymakers, journalists, students, and interested citizens in the United States and other countries, can better understand the world and the foreign policy choices facing the United States and other governments. The Council does this by convening meetings; conducting a wide-ranging Studies program; publishing *Foreign Affairs*, the preeminent journal covering international affairs and U.S. foreign policy; maintaining a diverse membership; sponsoring Independent Task Forces; and providing up-to-date information about the world and U.S. foreign policy on the Council's website, www.cfr.org.

THE COUNCIL TAKES NO INSTITUTIONAL POSITION ON POLICY ISSUES AND HAS NO AFFILIATION WITH THE U.S. GOVERNMENT. ALL STATEMENTS OF FACT AND EXPRESSIONS OF OPINION CONTAINED IN ITS PUBLICATIONS ARE THE SOLE RESPONSIBILITY OF THE AUTHOR OR AUTHORS.

The Council will sponsor an Independent Task Force when (1) an issue of current and critical importance to U.S. foreign policy arises, and (2) it seems that a group diverse in backgrounds and perspectives may, nonetheless, be able to reach a meaningful consensus on a policy through private and nonpartisan deliberations. Typically, a Task Force meets between two and five times over a brief period to ensure the relevance of its work.

Upon reaching a conclusion, a Task Force issues a report, and the Council publishes its text and posts it on the Council's website. Task Force reports can take three forms: (1) a strong and meaningful policy consensus, with Task Force members endorsing the general policy thrust and judgments reached by the group, though not necessarily every finding and recommendation; (2) a report stating the various policy positions, each as sharply and fairly as possible; or (3) a "Chairman's Report," where Task Force members who agree with the chairman's report may associate themselves with it, while those who disagree may submit dissenting statements. Upon reaching a conclusion, a Task Force may also ask individuals who were not members of the Task Force to associate themselves with the Task Force report to enhance its impact. All Task Force reports "benchmark" their findings against current administration policy in order to make explicit areas of agreement and disagreement. The Task Force is solely responsible for its report. The Council takes no institutional position.

For further information about the Council or this Task Force, please write to the Council on Foreign Relations, 58 East 68th Street, New York, NY 10021, or call the Director of Communications at 212-434-9400. Visit the Council's website at www.cfr.org.

TASK FORCE MEMBERS

---

*The individual has endorsed the report and submitted an additional or a dissenting view.

CONTENTS

FOREWORD

Over the past quarter century, relations between the United States and the Islamic Republic of Iran have been trapped by legacies of the past. The aftermath of the 1979 revolution transformed Iran from a staunch ally into one of the most intractable opponents of the United States in the region and beyond. Today, the wars in Afghanistan and Iraq have positioned American troops along Iran's borders, making the United States and Iran wary competitors and neighbors who nonetheless possess some overlapping interests. All of this is occurring against a backdrop of the problems posed by Iran's nuclear program and its involvement with terrorism. Clearly, contending with Iran will constitute one of the most complex and pressing challenges facing the next U.S. administration.

The Council on Foreign Relations established this Independent Task Force to consider both Iran's domestic reality and its foreign policy and to examine ways the United States can foster a relationship with Iran that better protects and promotes American interests in a critical part of the world.

The Task Force reaches the important assessment that "despite considerable political flux and popular dissatisfaction, Iran is not on the verge of another revolution." From this finding flows its advocacy of the United States adopting a policy of what it describes as limited or selective engagement with the current Iranian government.

The Council is deeply appreciative of two distinguished public servants, Dr. Zbigniew Brzezinski and Dr. Robert M. Gates, for chairing this effort. Their intellectual leadership steered this Task Force toward a consensus on an issue of great international importance. My thanks also go to Dr. Suzanne Maloney, a leading American expert on Iranian society, who skillfully directed this project from its inception. Finally, I wish to thank the members of this Task Force for this important contribution to the national debate.

Richard N. Haass
President
Council on Foreign Relations
July 2004

ACKNOWLEDGMENTS

The Independent Task Force on U.S. Policy toward Iran benefited greatly from the involvement of many individuals. First and foremost, we are indebted to the leadership of the chairs, Dr. Zbigniew Brzezinski and Dr. Robert M. Gates. Their judicious stewardship, broad intellectual vision, and vast experience framed this entire project.

From February to May 2004, Task Force members and observers participated in four meetings that took place at the Council on Foreign Relations in Washington, DC, and in New York. The discussions reflected the depth of the group's collective expertise on the subject matter at hand, as well as the wide range of their experiences in government, academia, business, and nongovernmental organizations. The willingness of all the participants to share ideas and offer suggestions on the report itself has greatly elevated the final product. In addition, several Council members outside of the Task Force generously contributed their time, interest, and perspectives on Iran. The report is richer as a result of their input.

Thanks go to Christopher Angell, a research associate at the Council, for his work in staffing the Task Force meetings, organizing material distributed to Task Force participants, and managing the many administrative details involved with this undertaking. We were also fortunate that one of the Council's military fellows, U.S. Navy Captain David Marquet, was involved as the project coordinator. Lindsay Workman and Abigail Zoba were both tremendous assets to the Task Force effort, and Lee Feinstein, the executive director of task forces at the Council, provided support and guidance throughout the process. We would also like to thank Sandy Crawford at Texas A&M University and Trudi Werner and Candice Wessling at the Center for Strategic and International Studies.

All those involved with this project are ultimately grateful to Richard N. Haass, president of the Council, who challenged the Task Force to think critically and carefully in examining the issues at stake.

Finally, the Task Force would not have been possible without the financial support of the Leonard and Evelyn Lauder Foundation and the Rockefeller Brothers Fund. We deeply appreciate their generosity.

Suzanne Maloney
Project Director

Note: Map courtesy of United Nations Cartographic Section: http://www.un.org/Depts/Cartographic/english/htmain.htm.

EXECUTIVE SUMMARY

Twenty-five years after its Islamic revolution, Iran represents a challenge and an opportunity for the United States. The issues at stake reflect the urgent and multifaceted dilemmas of U.S. security in the post-9/11 era: nuclear proliferation, state support of terrorism, the relationship between religion and politics, and the imperative of political and economic reform in the Middle East. At this time, as Iraq—Iran's neighbor and historic adversary—embarks on a difficult transition to post-conflict sovereignty, and as the International Atomic Energy Agency (IAEA) extends its scrutiny of Iranian nuclear activities, Iran looms large on the U.S. policy agenda. Recognizing this relevance to vital U.S. interests, the Task Force advocates selectively engaging with Iran to address critical U.S. concerns.

The Task Force centered its deliberations on Iran's domestic situation and overall foreign policy, in order to illuminate the context for U.S. policy. It did so in the recognition that the long absence of U.S. relations with Iran and Washington's limited ongoing contact with the country mean that any assessment of the internal dynamics of the Islamic Republic is inevitably imperfect. Nevertheless, it is the view of this Task Force that despite considerable political flux and popular dissatisfaction, Iran is not on the verge of another revolution. Those forces that are committed to preserving Iran's current system remain firmly in control and currently represent the country's only authoritative interlocutors. Direct U.S. efforts to overthrow the Iranian regime are therefore not likely to succeed; nor would regime change through external intervention necessarily resolve the most critical concerns with respect to Iran's policies. The ferment of recent years demonstrates that the Iranian people themselves will eventually change the nature of their government for the better. In the meantime, the durability of the Islamic Republic and the urgency of the concerns surrounding its policies mandate that the United States deal with the current regime rather than wait for it to fall.

U.S. concerns have long focused on Iran's activities and intentions toward its neighbors. Over the past decade, Iran's foreign policy has gradually acceded to the exigencies of national interest, except in certain crucial areas where ideology remains paramount. As a result, Tehran has reestablished largely constructive relations with its neighbors and has expanded international trade links. The changing regional context has produced new pressures and uncertainties for Iran. The Task Force concluded that although Iran's leadership is pursuing multiple avenues of influence and is exploiting Iraqi instability for its own political gain, Iran nevertheless could play a potentially significant role in promoting a stable, pluralistic government in Baghdad. It might be induced to be a constructive actor toward both Iraq and Afghanistan, but it retains the capacity to create significant difficulties for these regimes if it is alienated from the new post-conflict governments in those two countries.

The Task Force also reaffirms the proposition that one of the most urgent issues confronting the United States is Iran's nuclear ambitions. Although Task Force members voiced differing opinions on whether evidence is sufficient to determine that Iran has fully committed itself to developing nuclear weapons, the Task Force agreed that Iran is likely to continue its pattern of tactical cooperation with the International Atomic Energy Agency while attempting to conceal the scope of its nuclear program in order to keep its options open as long as possible.

At the core of the Task Force's conclusions is the recognition that it is in the interests of the United States to engage selectively with Iran to promote regional stability, dissuade Iran from pursuing nuclear weapons, preserve reliable energy supplies, reduce the threat of terror, and address the "democracy deficit" that pervades the Middle East as a whole. For these reasons, the members advocate a revised strategic approach to Iran.

A Revised Approach to Iran

The Task Force concluded that the current lack of sustained engagement with Iran harms U.S. interests in a critical region of the world and that direct dialogue with Tehran on specific areas of mutual concern should be pursued.

1.) A political dialogue with Iran should not be deferred until such a time as the deep differences over Iranian nuclear ambitions and its invidious involvement with regional conflicts have been resolved. Rather, the process of selective political engagement itself represents a potentially effective path for addressing those differences. Just as the United States maintains a constructive relationship with China (and earlier did so with the Soviet Union) while strongly opposing certain aspects of its internal and international policies, Washington should approach Iran with a readiness to explore areas of common interests, while continuing to contest objectionable policies. Ultimately, any real rapprochement with Tehran can only occur in the context of meaningful progress on the most urgent U.S. concerns surrounding nuclear weapons, terrorism, and regional stability.

2.) A "grand bargain" that would settle comprehensively the outstanding conflicts between Iran and the United States is not a realistic goal, and pursuing such an outcome would be unlikely to produce near-term progress on Washington's central interests. Instead, the Task Force proposes selectively engaging Iran on issues where U.S. and Iranian interests converge, and building upon incremental progress to tackle the broader range of concerns that divide the two governments.

3.) U.S. policies toward Tehran should make use of incentives as well as punitive measures. The U.S. reliance on comprehensive, unilateral sanctions has not succeeded in its stated objective to alter Iranian conduct and has deprived Washington of greater leverage vis-à-vis the Iranian government apart from the threat of force. Given the increasingly important role of economic interests in shaping Iran's policy options at home and abroad, the prospect of commercial relations with the United States could be a powerful tool in Washington's arsenal.

4.) The United States should advocate democracy in Iran without relying on the rhetoric of regime change, as that would be likely to rouse nationalist sentiments in defense of the current regime even among those who currently oppose it. The U.S. government should focus its rhetoric and its policies on promoting political evolution that encourages Iran to develop stronger democratic institutions at home and enhanced diplomatic and economic relations abroad. Engaging with the current government to address pressing regional and international issues need not contradict U.S. support for these objectives; indeed, engagement pursued judiciously would enhance the chances of internal change in Iran.

5.) The Task Force is mindful of repeated efforts over the last twenty-five years to engage the regime in Tehran, and that all of these have come to naught for various reasons. However, the Task Force believes that the U.S. military intervention along Iran's flanks in both Afghanistan and Iraq has changed the geopolitical landscape in the region. These changes may offer both the United States and Iran new incentives to open a mutually beneficial dialogue, first on issues of common interest, such as regional stability, and eventually on the tough issues of terrorism and proliferation. We recognize that even the most perspicacious policy toward Iran may be stymied by Iranian obstinacy.

Recommendations for U.S. Policy
In pursuit of the new approach outlined above, the Task Force recommends the following specific steps to address the most urgent issues of concern:

1.) The United States should offer Iran a direct dialogue on specific issues of regional stabilization. This should entail a resumption and expansion of the Geneva track discussions that were conducted with Tehran for eighteen months after the 9/11 attacks. The dialogue should be structured to encourage constructive Iranian involvement in the process of consolidating authority within the central governments of both Iraq and Afghanistan and in rebuilding their economies. Regular contact with Iran would also provide a channel to address concerns that have arisen about its activities and relationships with competing power centers in both countries. Instead of aspiring to a detailed road map of rapprochement, as previous U.S. administrations have recommended, the executive branch should consider outlining a more simple mechanism for framing formal dialogue with Iran. A basic statement of principles, along the lines of the 1972 Shanghai Communiqué signed by the United States and China, could be developed to outline the parameters for U.S.-Iranian engagement, establish the overarching objectives for dialogue, and reassure relevant domestic political constituencies on both sides. The effort to draft such a statement would give constructive focus and substance to a serious, but also realistic, bilateral dialogue. Should that effort end in stalemate, it should not preclude going forward with the dialogue on specific issues.

2.) The United States should press Iran to clarify the status of al-Qaeda operatives detained by Tehran and make clear that a security dialogue will be conditional on assurances that its government is not facilitating violence against the new Iraqi and Afghan governments or the coalition forces that are assisting them. At the same time, Washington should work with the interim government of Iraq to conclusively disband the Iraq-based Mojahideen-e Khalq Organization and ensure that its leaders are brought to justice.

3.) In close coordination with its allies in Europe and with Russia, the United States should implement a more focused strategy to deal with the Iranian nuclear program. In the immediate future, Iran should be pressed to fulfill its October 2003 commitment to maintain a complete and verified suspension of all enrichment-related and reprocessing activities. While this suspension is in effect, the United States and other members of the international community should pursue a framework agreement with Iran that would offer a more durable solution to the nuclear issue. Such an agreement should include an Iranian commitment to permanently renounce uranium enrichment and other fuel-cycle capabilities and to ratify the International Atomic Energy Agency's Additional Protocol, an expanded set of safeguards intended to verify the peaceful intentions of its nuclear program. In return, the United States should remove its objections to an Iranian civil nuclear program under stringent safeguards and assent to multilateral assurances that Tehran would be able to purchase fuel at reasonable market rates for nuclear power reactors as long as it abided by its nonproliferation commitments. The agreement should also commit both sides to enhancing political and economic relations, through a dialogue that would take place in parallel with Iran's established talks with the European Union.

In the short term, the United States should press the IAEA to exercise its Additional Protocol verification rights vigorously in order to deter and detect any clandestine nuclear activities. This should serve as a decisive test case for Iranian compliance with its obligations under Article II of the Nonproliferation Treaty and for the credibility and viability of the global nuclear nonproliferation regime. Tehran must clearly understand that unless it demonstrates real, uninterrupted cooperation with the IAEA process, it will face the prospect of multilateral sanctions imposed by the United Nations Security Council. Over the longer term, the United States should aim to convene a dialogue on issues of cooperative security involving Iran and its nuclear-armed neighbors.

4.) The United States should resume an active involvement in the Middle East peace process and press leading Arab states to commit themselves to providing genuine, substantive support for both the process and any ultimate agreements. Iranian incitement of virulent anti-Israeli sentiment and activities thrives when there is no progress toward peace. Efforts to curtail the flows of assistance to terrorist groups must be coupled with steps to offer a meaningful alternative to the continuing cycle of violence. A serious effort on the part of Washington aimed at achieving Arab-Israeli peace is central to eventually stemming the tide of extremism in the region.

5.) The United States should adopt measures to broaden the political, cultural, and economic linkages between the Iranian population and the wider world, including authorizing U.S. nongovernmental organizations to operate in Iran and consenting to Iran's application to begin accession talks with the World Trade Organization. Iran's isolation only impedes its people's ongoing struggle for a more democratic government and strengthens the hand of hard-liners who preach confrontation with the rest of the world. Integrating Iran into the international community through formal institutional obligations as well as expanded people-to-people contacts will intensify demands for good governance at home and add new constraints on adventurism abroad.

TASK FORCE REPORT

Introduction

The past two years have witnessed a series of extraordinary changes across the wider Middle East, a region long characterized by a dangerous status quo. Since the tragic turning point of 9/11, two governments whose threat to their citizens and their neighbors was well established—Afghanistan and Iraq—have been destroyed. In their place, a new set of strategic realities and opportunities has emerged.

To date, however, one U.S. policy problem in the Middle East has remained curiously impenetrable to the changes that have buffeted its neighbors: Iran. Nearly a quarter-century after the revolution that replaced a modernizing monarchy with a radical religious state that has abrogated a close alliance with Washington, U.S.-Iranian relations remain trapped by the legacies of the past and the very real differences of the present. These differences principally concern Iran's apparent efforts to acquire a nuclear weapons capability and its continuing support for militant groups involved in a variety of regional conflicts, including the Palestinian-Israeli dispute. But U.S. interests with respect to Iran go beyond these differences, important though they are, to include promoting democracy and prosperity in the Middle East and ensuring a stable flow of oil from the Persian Gulf.

In a region beset by turbulence and unpredictability, antagonism between Washington and Tehran has a curious constancy. The estrangement persists despite considerable internal change within the Islamic Republic since its chaotic postrevolutionary inception and despite the fact that the rift arguably undermines the interests of both states. However, dispassion remains a commodity in short supply in the Middle East, and Iran today endures as the only country in the region to categorically reject formal diplomatic relations with Washington.

Such durable antagonism might be sustainable in another part of the world, or in relations with another kind of state, but where Iran is concerned it is profoundly problematic. First, the rift defies the realities of this globalized era. As the most populous country in the Middle East and one of the world's leading energy producers, Iran today cannot enjoy the luxury of wholesale recalcitrance and isolationism as pursued by rogue states such as North Korea. By the same token, Iran's intrinsic involvement with its neighbors and with the global political and financial order limits the efficacy of any U.S. policy of outright isolation or simple disinterest.

Moreover, the official enmity between Washington and Tehran belies the convergence of their interests in specific areas. The strategic imperatives of the United States and Iran are by no means identical, nor are they often even congruent, but they do intersect in significant ways, particularly with respect to the stabilization of Iraq and Afghanistan. In regard to both these countries, the short-term needs and long-term visions of Washington and Tehran are surprisingly similar. Although they may differ profoundly on specifics, both the United States and Iran want post-conflict governments in Iraq and Afghanistan that respect the rights of their diverse citizenries and live in peace with their neighbors. The hostility that characterizes U.S.-Iranian relations undermines these shared interests and squanders the potential benefits of even limited cooperation. As tenuous new governments in Baghdad and Kabul embark on precarious post-conflict futures, the United States and the region cannot afford to spurn any prospective contributions to the region's stability.

Finally, the estrangement has tended to further entrench some of the very policies that are sources of conflict between the United States and Iran. The frustrating but familiar interplay between Tehran and Washington has generated a self-perpetuating cycle whereby mutual distrust begets uncompromising assertiveness and unyielding negotiating positions. Tehran's nuclear programs are driven in part by aspirations for an ultimate deterrent against any threat to its national security; these efforts, in turn, stiffen U.S. resolve to mobilize an international consensus in opposition to Iran's policies. Overcoming the absence of any U.S.-Iranian contacts may be the only alternative to utilizing force in mitigating Washington's major concerns about Iran's behavior.

The Task Force was challenged to examine the issues at stake with respect to Iran and to propose a future course to best address U.S. concerns and advance U.S. interests. At the core of this effort is an overarching conviction that Iran poses a complex and compelling set of concerns for many important U.S. security interests, particularly curbing terrorism and checking the proliferation of weapons of mass destruction. The report begins with an overview of these interests, offers an assessment of the general trends shaping Iranian internal politics and international relations, and analyzes the critical areas of proliferation and regional conflict. Finally, it offers the assessments and recommendations of the Task Force for dealing with these challenges.

WHY IRAN MATTERS

The United States is currently engaged in a vast region encompassing the Middle East and Central Asia to an extent unprecedented in its history. This region is complicated, volatile, and vitally important to an array of U.S. geostrategic interests. Iran occupies a central position—literally and symbolically—in the Middle East, and as such its internal and international conduct have wide-ranging repercussions for the region as a whole and for U.S. interests within it.

Consider Iran's environs. To the east is a fractious Afghanistan that is the fountainhead of chaos fueled by religion and drugs. To the southeast is Pakistan, a nuclear-armed state that may be on the verge of another ethno-religious explosion. To the northeast is Turkmenistan, whose erratic communist ruler has isolated his country from the world. Across Iran's northwest border is Azerbaijan, with a government still navigating the challenges of post-Soviet transition. Also to the northwest is Turkey, the single successful democracy in the Muslim Middle East and, if it joins the European Union, a potential border with the West. To the west is Iran's historic adversary, Iraq, occupied by 140,000 U.S. troops and currently in turmoil. Finally, to Iran's south and southeast lie the vulnerable Gulf sheikhdoms, its regional rival Saudi Arabia, and the passageways through which 40 percent of the world's oil must flow.

Iran thus lies at the heart of the arc of crisis in the Middle East. Its intricate political, cultural, and economic ties to Afghanistan and Iraq—including long-standing involvement with opposition movements that have worked with Washington to establish successor governments in each country—make Iran a critical actor in the postwar evolution of both countries. Its large endowment of natural resources—approximately 11 percent of the world's oil reserves and the second-largest deposits of natural gas—positions Iran as an indispensable player in the world economy. Its status as the largest Shia state and heir to the first religious revolution in modern times means it heavily influences wider doctrinal debates surrounding Islamic governance and jurisprudence. Finally, Iran's long history as a cohesive state with a tradition of constitutionalism and experience in representative government means that its political experience may prove a valuable model for any regional transition to a more democratic order.

Two recent developments highlight the most urgent priorities for U.S. policy toward Iran. The first was the decision by the International Atomic Energy Agency (IAEA) at its June 14–16, 2004, board of governors meeting to rebuke Iran for failing to cooperate adequately with the organization's investigation into its nuclear program. The latest IAEA report, based on an inquiry launched more than two years ago and intensified by a series of revelations concerning Iran's clandestine nuclear activities, illustrates the complexities that the international community faces in contending with Iranian resourcefulness and diplomatic dexterity in covering for its extensive nuclear activities. It also highlights the need for the West to develop an effective strategy for countering Iranian proliferation efforts.

Beyond the nuclear imbroglio, the evolving situation in Iraq also underscores the vital relevance of Iran for U.S. policy there. As Iraq navigates its recent transfer from international occupation to limited sovereignty, the prospects for its short- and long-term stability hinge to a considerable extent on the role of its neighbors. By virtue of its history and geography as well as its intricate religious ties to Iraq, Iran has and will continue to bear unique influence over the transition to a post–Saddam Hussein Iraqi political order. Given the centrality of success in Iraq to the United States' broader international objectives, the U.S. government has an important stake in ensuring that the role of Iran in the future evolution of Iraq is a positive one.

IRAN'S DOMESTIC DILEMMAS

Ultimately, any U.S. policy toward Tehran must be conditioned by a credible assessment of the current regime's durability. The breach between the countries began with a revolution, and many argue that it cannot conclusively end without another comprehensive transformation in the nature and composition of the Iranian government. Moreover, recent political ferment within Iran and expectations of a demonstration effect from regime change in Iraq has given rise to persistent anticipation that such a revolution is imminent. Although largely overly optimistic, these forecasts have helped shape U.S. policy toward Tehran, conditioning the administration of George W. Bush to reach out to putative opposition leaders and making U.S. policymakers reluctant to engage with the current regime in order to avoid perpetuating its hold on power.

Inevitably, the distance established by geography and political separation complicates any accurate understanding of Iran's domestic politics today. Still, certain broad conclusions can be drawn from a careful consideration of the recent patterns of politics in Iran. Most important, the Islamic Republic appears to be solidly entrenched and the country is not on the brink of revolutionary upheaval. Iran is experiencing a gradual process of internal change that will slowly but surely produce a government more responsive toward its citizens' wishes and more responsible in its approach to the international community. In contrast to all of its neighbors—and to the prevailing stereotypes inculcated by its own vitriolic rhetoric—Iran is home to vigorous, albeit restricted, political competition and a literate, liberalizing society. Even after the recent political setbacks, Iran today remains a state in which political factions compete with one another within an organized system, restrictions on civil rights and social life are actively contested, and the principles of authority and power are debated energetically.

Although Iran's political competition and debate are robust, however, they nevertheless exist within the narrowly defined constraints imposed on the country by its unique governing framework, which accords ultimate power to unelected and unaccountable Islamic clerics, culminating in the Supreme Leader Ayatollah Ali Khamenei. Under this regime, the Iranian government enforces severe restrictions on all aspects of political, cultural, and economic life, and routinely violates even those limited protections enacted in its own constitution and laws. The restricted scope of Iran's electoral politics was made only too clear in recent parliamentary elections, held in February 2004, in which a clerical oversight body disqualified more than 3,000 candidates from competing, including eighty then members of the parliament.

Iran's theocratic system is deeply unpopular with its citizenry. In their own media as well as in dialogue with external interlocutors, many Iranians—across a wide spectrum of age, class, and ethnic and religious backgrounds—are candid and scathing in their criticism of their government and its policies. Iranians also expressed this criticism through a series of surprising electoral outcomes in the late 1990s that, even within the narrow limits of permissible politics, indicated resounding support for progressive reform of the governing system. Large-scale demonstrations are rare due to fear of repression, but they have surfaced intermittently and with great intensity in various parts of the country. Most notable were the July 1999 and June 2003 student protests, both of which were violently crushed by government security forces.

A central factor in Iran's political agitation is the coming of age of a new generation of Iranians whose expectations and sense of political entitlement has been framed by their rearing under the revolution. Young people comprise as much as 70 percent of the population and are positioned to serve as arbiters of the country's political order in the near future. Generally speaking, young Iranians are highly literate, well educated, and supportive of expanded social and cultural liberties and political participation. Given that approximately one-third of young job-seekers are unemployed, economic interests rank high on their list of political priorities.

With the disqualification of liberal-minded candidates from Iran's 2004 parliamentary elections, the country's reform movement has effectively been sidelined as a significant actor in formulating domestic or international policy. Reformist leaders were largely unwilling to challenge the basic parameters of Islamic politics and their organization, which includes nascent political parties such as the Islamic Iran Participation Front, and proved unable to mount an effective bid for change. As a result, the reform movement's central strategy—gradual change brought about from within the existing governing system—has been discredited by Iranian citizens as a viable pathway to reform. As a June 2004 report by Human Rights Watch details, Iran's conservative forces quashed efforts to promote peaceful political change with a deft strategy of silencing public debate and eliminating potential opposition leaders.

Still, the influence of reformers—both as individuals and through the articulation of their ideas—remains notable, albeit indirect. The reform movement has had an important role in shaping public expectations and in setting the context for future change, and future leaders of any post–Islamic Republic political movement will likely come from reformers' diverse ranks. The Task Force anticipates that just as these people emanated from the alienated ranks of the early revolution, the students, journalists, and political actors who have been frustrated in their attempts to implement gradual reform may now redirect their efforts to mobilize public support to press for fundamental changes to the political system.

Conservatives and hard-liners who are committed to the preservation of the Islamic Republic's status quo remain firmly in control of all institutions and instruments of power in Iran. They represent the locus of power and the only authoritative interlocutors for any diplomatic interface. Although some may be amenable to limited moderation of Iranian policies and rhetoric, conservatives have repeatedly demonstrated their willingness to preserve the regime by crushing anti-regime protests and imprisoning or even killing their political opponents.

Yet despite their commitment to retaining the current system (and, in part, because of that very factor), at least some segments of Iran's conservative faction, such as former President Ali Akbar Hashemi Rafsanjani, are capable of making limited concessions to reform in their policies both at home and abroad. Conservatives' overriding interest in retaining power means that they have an increasing imperative to avoid provoking international tensions, so as to preserve and expand the economic opportunities available to Iran in general and to their own privileged elite cohort in particular. Some conservatives appear to favor a "China model" of reform that maintains political orthodoxy while encouraging market reforms and tolerating expanding civil liberties.

For this reason, Iran's economy offers an ever more important avenue of potential influence by outsiders. High global oil prices have boosted the overall growth rates of the Iranian economy, but structural distortions—including massive subsidies, endemic corruption, a disproportionately large public sector, and dependency on oil rents—severely undermine the strength of the Iranian economy. Iran's economic woes pose direct, daily hardships for its population, whose income measured on a per capita basis has fallen by approximately one-third since the revolution. With as many as one million new job-seekers coming into the market each year, the single greatest challenge for any government in Iran will be generating conditions for job growth. Iran needs a substantial and sustained expansion of private investment sufficient for its productive capacity, including as much as $18 billion per year in foreign direct investment, in order to meet these demands.

Iran's conservatives tout their capabilities to address these economic challenges, but in fact neither they nor their rivals can boast a successful track record on the economy. This is due, in part, to the political sensitivities that are invoked by the prospect of sound economic development. Real reform would effectively undermine the power of the state and the monopoly enjoyed by Iran's elites. Creating a secure climate for foreign investment, meanwhile, would necessitate a more accommodating international posture. Ultimately, economic reform in Iran would promote more responsible governance at home and abroad. Unfortunately, however, high oil prices have enabled Tehran to defer these politically painful steps.

Following a brief period of increased political ferment in the late 1990s, Iran's public has become intensely disillusioned with both the status quo and available political alternatives and has become manifestly disengaged from the political process itself. They have shunned the reform movement (most recently by delivering it a surprising defeat in 2003 municipal elections) and are increasingly frank in their outright rejection of any political formula that retains the current theocratic system.

Despite this widespread alienation from the prevailing political order, Iran does not now appear to be in a prerevolutionary situation. Iranians are protesting the political system by withholding their participation from any form of organized politics, including involvement with the opposition. People are frustrated with the Islamic Republic, but they have also demonstrated that they are not yet prepared to take that frustration to the streets. This disengagement from politics is a direct product of Iran's recent history. Having endured the disappointment of their last democratic experiment gone awry, Iranians are weary of political turmoil and skeptical that they can positively change their political circumstances through mass mobilization.

Moreover, to date, no organization or potential leader has emerged with the apparent discipline or stamina to sustain a major confrontation with the government's conservative forces. Several national student organizations, such as the Office for the Consolidation of Unity (*Daftar-e Takhim-e Vahdat*), are vocal proponents of democratic change, but government repression has muted their effectiveness.

As a result of these factors, the current Iranian government appears to be durable and likely to persist in power for the short and even medium term. However, Iran's generational shift and prevailing popular frustration with the government portend the eventual transformation to a more democratic political order in the long term. That process is too deeply entrenched in Iran's political history and social structure to be derailed or even long delayed.

IRAN'S APPROACH TO THE WORLD

Throughout the history of the Islamic Republic, Iran's domestic dynamics have had a direct impact on its foreign policy agenda and approach. In the past, factional infighting has precipitated some of the most provocative elements of its foreign policy, such as the 1979 seizure of the U.S. embassy, the 1989 promulgation of a *fatwa* condemning writer Salman Rushdie to death, and the more recent "Dialogue Among Civilizations" initiative. Today, internal rivalries continue to infiltrate Iran's external activities, and, as a result, Iran's many official institutions often pursue policies in direct contradiction with one another.

Over the course of the past twenty-five years, Iran's foreign policy has moderated in significant and meaningful ways. Whereas the Islamic Republic initially repudiated the prevailing norms of the international system, today its government has largely abandoned its efforts to topple the region's existing political order and approaches interstate relations primarily on the basis of national interest rather than ideology. In seeking to project its influence and protect its interests, the Islamic Republic has increasingly yielded to realist principles. Today, Iran's foreign policy exhibits striking extremes of accommodation and antagonism.

Commercial considerations figure prominently in the realignment of Iranian foreign policy. Iran's interests in maintaining and expanding international trade, attracting foreign direct investment, and coordinating oil policy with other leading producers to prevent a future price collapse have shaped its approach to the world and conditioned its partial abandonment of confrontational tactics in favor of a more accommodating stance.

These broad contours of Iranian foreign policy are evident in its successful implementation of detente with its neighbors in the southern Persian Gulf, in its pragmatic approach to its northern neighbors in the Caucasus and Central Asia, and in its cultivation of close ties with a range of regional actors, including India, Russia, China, Japan, and the European Union. This last effort is designed to offset Iran's persistent official antagonism with the United States.

Tehran's approach to Washington remains one of several decisive exceptions to the general trend toward moderation and realism in Iranian foreign policy. In formulating Iranian policy toward the United States, ideological imperatives continue to outweigh dispassionate calculations of national interest. Iran's strident opposition to Israel is also the product of self-defeating dogma. These exceptions may be slowly abated by the erosion of Iran's revolutionary orthodoxies, the growing importance of public support as a component of regime legitimacy, and the increasing difficulty of international integration. Nonetheless, for the immediate future,

Iranian foreign policy remains a captive of the regime's official enshrinement of anti-American and anti-Israeli ideology.

The general framework for Iranian foreign policy has remained relatively consistent over the past several years, and is likely to continue to do so in the near future. Moreover, there is a growing consensus within Iran's foreign policy elite around the principal pillars of its strategic interests. Steps that heretofore were ideologically taboo—such as the still-incomplete normalization of relations with Egypt, whose government sheltered the deposed shah and signed a peace treaty with Israel—today command broad-based support among most factions in Iranian politics.

Recent shifts in Iran's domestic political fortunes may facilitate enhanced flexibility and coherence in its foreign policy. The recent setbacks for Iranian reformers have reconsolidated the official organs in the hands of a single ideological faction. Although they have historically pandered to anti-American sentiments, Iran's conservatives have also demonstrated a track record of success in crafting compromise approaches and following through with their implementation. The pragmatists who appear to be ascendant in Tehran have described dialogue with the United States as a course that is "neither wine, nor prayer"—in other words, neither prohibited nor obligatory.

The prospects for additional moderation of Iran's international approach remain highly uncertain, however. The strengthened position of Iranian conservatives at home may inspire some to restoke ideological fires abroad in order to reinvigorate their domestic constituencies and justify extremist policies. An inflated sense of their own bargaining power may constrain the conservatives' willingness to moderate their own international conduct and could well lead them to anticipate disproportionate rewards for any cooperation.

IRAN'S NUCLEAR PROGRAMS

Over the past two years, Iran's construction of extensive uranium-enrichment facilities was made evident through the work of Iranian opposition groups and follow-up inquiries by the International Atomic Energy Agency. The disclosures of the hitherto underclared research facilities in Natanz and Tehran together with a heavy-water production plant in Arak, and the acknowledgement of significant imports of uranium from China, transformed the urgency of intelligence estimates surrounding Iran's nuclear capabilities and reduced the time remaining before it may reach a nuclear threshold. These discoveries, and the string of alarming revelations that have emerged through subsequent IAEA inspections, have also given rise to new doubts about the credibility of the Iranian commitment to abide by the terms of the Nuclear Nonproliferation Treaty (NPT). The revelations about the extent of Iran's nuclear program have confirmed U.S. suspicions and have transformed the assessments of others. According to the IAEA, Iran has achieved "a practically complete front end of a nuclear fuel cycle,"[1] and considerable evidence suggests that this is part of a multipronged effort to acquire and/or produce fissile material. Exacerbating concern about Iran's nuclear activities is its long-established and sophisticated missile development program, which has successfully produced medium-range missiles capable of targeting regional states such as Israel. Tehran also has plans for intercontinental ballistic missiles.

The Bush administration responded to these developments with a combination of tough rhetoric and concerted international pressure. The alarming nature of the disclosures helped to generate a rare multilateral consensus aligned to admonish Iran, as did the coincidental emergence of new irritants in Iran's previously smooth relations with Canada and Argentina—whose governments each

---

[1] "Implementation of the NPT Safeguards Agreement in the Islamic Republic of Iran," Report by the Director General of the International Atomic Energy Agency, November 10, 2003.

currently serve on the board of the IAEA. The outcome was an unprecedented effort by the international community to exert increased pressure on Iran concerning its nuclear activities, an effort underlined by the implicit threat of United Nations Security Council action and the potential for international economic sanctions.

This multilateral pressure generated noteworthy short-term progress, with an October 2003 Iranian agreement to sign the Additional Protocol mandating enhanced verification of both declared and undeclared materials and activities. The Iranians also agreed to suspend enrichment-related and reprocessing activities. The agreement was negotiated by the United Kingdom, France, and Germany, whose foreign ministers committed their governments to providing Iran access to peaceful nuclear technology. The agreement represented a limited but meaningful concession by Iran, one that reportedly evoked contentious debates among its senior leadership. At the time, it also offered a compromise that met the immediate interests of both the United States and its allies when neither side wished to repeat the acrimony that had emerged only a year earlier over Iraq. Subsequent Iranian statements and actions have significantly diminished confidence regarding Iran's intentions to abide by the terms of this deal, however. The October accord and Iran's subsequent interaction with the IAEA represent an inherently ephemeral victory in what must be, by definition, an open-ended relationship between the Iranian government and the international community on nuclear issues. Since that time, Iran's interaction with the IAEA has been characterized by continued friction, obfuscation, and a steady flow of new revelations about the true extent of Iranian nuclear activities. The recent diversion of nuclear materials to Iran has raised expectations of further confrontations in the future.

The IAEA has continued to walk a fine line, maintaining pressure on Tehran while avoiding provoking either further Iranian intransigence or a breakdown in the hard-won consensus among its own members. During a March 2004 visit to Washington, IAEA Director General Mohammad ElBaradei reiterated frankly that "the jury is still out" on the status of Iran's nuclear program—as well as on the extent of the clerical regime's preparedness to abide fully by its agreements to disclose all aspects of that program.[2] In June 2004, the IAEA board of governors passed its most strongly worded resolution to date, drawing attention to Iran's failure to cooperate in a timely manner, the omissions in its disclosures to the international community, and the urgency surrounding the most problematic elements of Iran's nuclear program. The IAEA and the international community appear to be converging around the conclusion articulated by the Bush administration more than a year ago that Iran has not complied with its obligations under the NPT. In response, Tehran announced that it would resume construction of centrifuges in contravention of its earlier pledges in the October accord.

Iran's Nuclear Imperatives

Given its history and its turbulent neighborhood, Iran's nuclear ambitions do not reflect a wholly irrational set of strategic calculations. Arguments for enhancing Iran's nuclear capabilities are necessarily pursued in private more often than in public forums, although the recent diplomatic activities vis-à-vis the IAEA have to some extent provoked a more freely available debate. Nonetheless, the rationale behind Iran's pursuit of a nuclear option can be elucidated from the rich literature on security issues that is present in Iranian academic journals and the press. Despite the clerics' frequent rhetorical invocations referencing the Israeli nuclear capability, this is not one of the primary drivers for Iran's own program. Rather, in addition to the prodigious sense of insecurity inculcated by the Iraqi invasion and the experience of the war itself, there appears to be widespread consensus surrounding two other important consequences of weapons of mass destruction: prestige and leverage. The former reflects the deeply held national pride that is a distinctly Iranian characteristic; it is simply inconceivable to

---

[2] Transcript, CNN, March 18, 2004.

Iranians across the political spectrum that neighboring Pakistan, a country considered to be exponentially inferior in terms of its economy, society, and political maturity, should have access to more advanced military technology. The second factor that pervades Iranian consideration of its nuclear options, leverage, further exposes the fundamental strategic deficiencies of Iran's continuing estrangement from the United States. For many in Tehran, maintaining some sort of viable nuclear program offers the single most valuable enhancement of the country's bargaining position with Washington.

The elimination of Saddam Hussein's regime has unequivocally mitigated one of Iran's most serious security concerns. Yet regime change in Iraq has left Tehran with potential chaos along its vulnerable western borders, as well as with an ever more proximate U.S. capability for projecting power in the region. By contributing to heightened tensions between the Bush administration and Iran, the elimination of Saddam's rule has not yet generated substantial strategic dividends for Tehran. In fact, together with U.S. statements on regime change, rogue states, and preemptive action, recent changes in the regional balance of power have only enhanced the potential deterrent value of a "strategic weapon."

Unlike Iran's other provocative policies, which have provoked intrafactional debate and thereby played into the internal power struggle in the country, the nuclear temptation is widely shared across the Iranian political spectrum. It dates back to the prerevolutionary period, when the monarchy began developing a nuclear program that was ostensibly for power generation purposes but understood to be intended as a launch pad for an ongoing weapons research effort. Opponents of crossing the nuclear threshold remain vocal and influential. Still, it is clear that the nuclear potential resonates with a collective set of interests that do not neatly correspond with Iran's political factions. The prestige factor and the apparent deterrent that a nuclear capability represents will offer powerful incentives for an Iranian regime of any political character.

As has become increasingly evident in the more public debate of the past several months, however, Iran's political elites are divided by a subordinate (but still critical) issue: the prospect of confrontation with the international community over a nascent nuclear weapons capability. Although reformers emphasize the benefits of Iran's regional detente and its commercial relations with Europe and Asia, hard-liners are not deterred by the prospect of international sanctions and isolation and would welcome a crisis as a means of rekindling Iran's waning revolutionary fires and deflecting attention from the domestic deficiencies of Islamic rule.

Iran's Nuclear Future

A number of uncertainties surrounding Iran's nuclear program remain outstanding. First, the viability of the October agreement between Iran and the three European foreign ministers remains in considerable doubt, particularly given Iran's recent decision to resume centrifuge construction. This defiant step by Tehran is the latest bid to erode the original terms of the agreement, as well as to undermine the narrow consensus that was attained between Europe and the United States on the issue. Iran's leadership appears to be trying to maintain momentum in its nuclear program while avoiding a major confrontation with the international community. Iran's commitments in the October accord were in fact quite expansive, entailing a complete suspension of all enrichment-related and reprocessing activities—originally understood to include production of centrifuge parts, assembly and testing of centrifuges, and production of uranium hexaflouride feedstock—and of the construction of a heavy-water reactor. The primary challenge for the international community today is formulating an effective response to Iran's efforts to flout its October 2003 promises.

In addition, there are a number of outstanding subordinate issues. Ratification of the Additional Protocol by the Iranian parliament has still not happened (the issue was expected to be taken up some time after the May 2004 inauguration of representatives who won their seats in the extremely flawed February balloting that produced an overwhelming conservative majority). Although Iran has promised to provisionally apply the protocol in advance of ratification, as required by its agreement with the IAEA, the parliamentary debate (and the need for subsequent endorsement by the hard-line Council of Guardians) leaves open an opportunity for Iran to hedge or renege on its commitments.

Also unresolved is a long-promised deal between Tehran and Moscow on the return of spent nuclear fuel from Bushehr, although both sides have said repeatedly that such an accord is imminent. Russia has particular reason for concern about Iran's ultimate ambitions in this regard, since success in Iran's efforts to produce nuclear fuel would obviate the need to purchase Russian supplies of fresh fuel. Russia and Iran also remain in protracted negotiations concerning the possibility of developing a second power plant at Bushehr.

Finally, even if it were to fulfill its commitments under the NPT and the Additional Protocol to the letter, Iran would still possess the legal and technical capabilities to establish an elaborate nuclear infrastructure with significant applicability for military purposes. Under its international treaty obligations, Iran is permitted to enrich uranium, construct heavy-water plants, and complete an indigenous fuel cycle. Moreover, the sophisticated nature of its capabilities reveals that Iran is approaching the point of self-sufficiency, where external assistance will no longer be required to acquire a weapon capability. Should Iran reach that threshold, traditional counter-proliferation measures are unlikely to affect its nuclear timetable. Given that Iranian officials have pledged to resume its uranium-enrichment activities once the IAEA verification is complete, the October accord may have only furnished Iran with a new delaying tactic as it inches closer to full-fledged nuclear weapons status.

Iran's recent conduct indicates that the government is likely to continue pursuing a sort of selective accommodation with the international community on the nuclear issue, yielding to additional inspections while continuing activities that advance its military options.

This may extend to maintaining a clandestine nuclear program for military aims in parallel with its declared civilian activities, as alleged by an exiled Iranian opposition group. At a minimum, Iran's pattern of concealment and the sophisticated and extensive nature of its disclosed activities indicate that its leadership is committed to retaining all available nuclear options. As a result, the real imperative for the United States will be to maintain consensus around a continuing effort to check Iranian progress toward a nuclear weapons capability within the broad international coalition erected over the last year.

INVOLVEMENT WITH REGIONAL CONFLICTS

Three regional issues have emerged as the centerpiece of the Bush administration's Middle East policy: stabilizing Iraq and Afghanistan and resolving the Israeli-Palestinian conflict. Iran has major influence in all three arenas and can potentially play an important role in assisting or retarding Washington's objectives. U.S. policy pronouncements concerning Iranian involvement in each sphere tend to reduce its role to generalized allegations of terrorism; however, the reality is more complex, particularly with respect to post-conflict Iraq and Afghanistan.

Iran has arguably benefited more than any other country from U.S. policies toward the Middle East since September 11, 2001. By removing the Taliban and Saddam Hussein from power in Afghanistan and Iraq, Washington has eliminated two of Tehran's most bitter enemies and most serious threats. What has replaced them, however, is not unambiguously preferable from Iran's point of view, as the new regional landscape entails profound uncertainties, new geographic proximity with the United States, and the threat (and, to some extent, reality) of chaos.

The Iranian government has often played a constructive and unheralded role in U.S.-led efforts to establish effective institutions of central government authority in Iraq and Afghanistan. At the same time, Iranians have cultivated ties with a wide range of political actors in both countries, including extremists, as a means of maximizing their potential leverage. This cultivation has taken place via both official and informal mechanisms and ranges from the direct recognition and assistance provided to the central government in each country to financial and material support funneled to bad actors bent on subverting the nascent democratic processes under way. As a result of its compelling strategic interest in retaining influence over the dramatic evolution of its immediate neighbors, Iran's multilevel approach to Iraq and Afghanistan is certain to continue.

Afghanistan and Al-Qaeda
Enmity between the Taliban and Iran long predated the events of September 11, 2001, that precipitated the U.S. military campaign in Afghanistan. Iranian suspicions of the Taliban movement were present from the outset, engendered by its origins in the radical Sunni seminaries of Pakistan and its close association with Islamabad's military and intelligence services. Ever concerned with the country's stature as an Islamic state and vulnerable to a distinctive Persian pride, Iranian officials viewed the Taliban as reactionary peasants sullying the image of Islam. Their animosity was exacerbated by the rising tide of drugs and instability from Taliban-controlled Afghanistan that too frequently spilled across the Iranian border. For the Taliban's part, their extreme ascetic doctrine reviled Shia Muslims as apostates, and its militants menaced Afghanistan's Shia minority. Tensions between the neighbors nearly escalated to direct conflict in August 1998, after eleven Iranian diplomats were murdered in the Taliban takeover of a Shia city. As a result, Iran cultivated close ties to the opposition militias that were battling the Taliban, including the Northern Alliance.

This history positioned Iran as an unlikely ally in the post-9/11 campaign by the United States to unseat the Taliban and deny safe haven in Afghanistan to al-Qaeda. Iran's early track record was extremely promising: Tehran continued to work in tandem with the

U.S. military effort in Afghanistan through the Northern Alliance, and it played an active and constructive role in the Bonn process that produced a new central government in post-conflict Kabul. Iranian officials also point to Iran's extensive logistical efforts to facilitate the U.S. victory over the Taliban, and its considerable aid to, and early recognition of, the post-conflict administration organized under President Hamid Karzai.

The Bush administration has acknowledged these efforts but has also consistently pointed to the more nefarious elements of Iranian actions in Afghanistan. As early as January 2002, President Bush issued a thinly veiled warning to Iran against any interference in Afghanistan, stating, "If they, in any way, shape, or form, try to destabilize the government, the coalition will deal with them . . . in diplomatic ways, initially."[3] Senior administration officials have often criticized Iran's involvement with Afghan warlords whose independent power bases contribute to the lack of stability and tenuous nature of central government authority today.

It is critical to consider recent allegations of collusion between Iranian hard-liners and al-Qaeda. These allegations contravene both the Islamic Republic's accommodating stance toward the 2001 U.S. military campaign in Afghanistan and the well-established track record of hostility between Iran and al-Qaeda's ascetic strand of Sunni militancy. Al-Qaeda's ideology and worldview are unrelentingly opposed to the Shia branch of Islam, which its theologians brand as a heretical sect. Nonetheless, both al-Qaeda's operational leadership and the radical hard-liners who dominate the senior ranks of Iran's security bureaucracy have demonstrated in the past a certain degree of doctrinal flexibility that has facilitated functional alliances, irrespective of apparent ideological incompatibility.

The allegations of cooperation between al-Qaeda and Iran are shrouded by the lack of much verifiable public evidence. Some reports suggest that militants associated with al-Qaeda

---

[3] U.S. Department of State, International Information Programs, "Bush Says Iran Must Contribute to War against Terror, Expresses Hope Iran Will Help Stabilize Afghanistan," January 10, 2002.

have had direct contacts with Iranian officials since the mid-1990s; however, no serious reports demonstrate substantive cooperation prior to the 9/11 attacks. More disturbing is evidence that since the attacks Iran has served as a transit route for, and has possibly offered safe harbor to, al-Qaeda operatives fleeing Afghanistan, including several prominent leaders such as spokesman Suleiman Abu Ghaith and security chief Saif Al Adel. Related to these allegations are reports that Imad Mughniyeh, the head of Hezbollah's special operations directorate and one of Washington's most wanted terrorist suspects, has also found sanctuary in Iran.

When public criticism by the U.S. government on this issue intensified after early 2002, Iran confirmed that it had detained an unspecified number of individuals connected with al-Qaeda and later acknowledged that these operatives included both "small- and big-time elements." The circumstances of their entry into Iran are not publicly known, nor are any details of their status beyond the announced Iranian intention to put the al-Qaeda representatives on trial. Iran also claims to have deported at least 500 individuals who fled Afghanistan on the heels of the U.S. military campaign. Although Iran has trumpeted these actions as evidence of its vigilance in countering al-Qaeda's domestic and international threat, U.S. concerns about Iran's posture intensified after the May 2003 attacks on expatriate housing complexes in Saudi Arabia that were attributed to al-Qaeda operatives, possibly working from Iran. As a result, Washington suspended the quiet constructive dialogue between the two governments that had developed after 9/11 on a limited range of regional issues.

The nature of Iran's relationship with al-Qaeda is subject to innuendo and interpretation. Its eastern borders are notoriously porous, as Iranian officials are prone to noting in its defense. However, even if this is true, Iran's opaque handling of its unwelcome guests strains credulity. One plausible, although as yet unverified, explanation is that Iran's reluctance to turn over captured al-Qaeda operatives stems from concerns that such cooperation could produce evidence of complicity between Iranian hard-liners and individual terrorists. Behind the scenes, Iranian officials have suggested exchanging its al-Qaeda detainees for members of the Mojahideen-e Khalq Organization, who are currently interned by U.S. occupying forces in Iraq. Like many other episodes in the history of its turbulent relationship with Washington, Iran's insistence on clinging to what it perceives to be a valuable bargaining chip may lead to an overestimation of its potential leverage and an ultimate weakening of its own security.

Iraq

As with the Taliban, Iran's long track record of conflict with Saddam Hussein is well established. The eight-year Iran-Iraq War was so bitter and exhausting that it did not end in a formal peace treaty and relations between the two countries did not fully resume for the ensuing sixteen years of Saddam's rule. Here, too, Tehran and Washington found themselves improbably united by a common enemy, although the problematic history of U.S. policy toward Iraq and the implicit threat of Iran's affiliation with its Shia majority added considerable layers of complexity and wariness. In the lead-up to the 2003 campaign by the U.S.-led coalition to remove Saddam Hussein, Iranian officials opposed the War was in the most robust terms, mindful of the precedent that would be set and the fact that the U.S. military would be parked on Iran's western border. In private conversations, Iranians offered their own tragic experience in Iraq as an admonition against any optimism about the prospects for a positive post-conflict scenario.

In the immediate aftermath of the coalition victory, however, Iran also recognized an unprecedented opportunity to extend its own influence and encourage the ascension of a friendly fellow Shia government. As a result, Iran sanctioned cooperation with the U.S. occupation via one of its primary instruments for projecting power in Iraq: the Shia opposition groups. In particular, the Supreme Council for the Islamic Revolution in Iraq, which has long-standing and intricate ties to Iran's governing clergy, emerged as a central and constructive actor in the nascent politics of post-

Saddam Iraq. In addition, Iran offered early recognition to the precarious provisional government and quickly launched efforts to expand economic and cultural ties with Iraqis.

Just as in Afghanistan, however, Iran's cooperation did not negate U.S. concerns about its leaders' ultimate intentions and its potential for undertaking subversive activities. Tehran reportedly tested the commitment of the occupying forces to preserving Iraq's existing borders, briefly moving across the south-central border in the summer of 2003. Iran's clerical forces also began reaching out to a wide variety of Iraqi organizations and leaders, including militants such as Moqtada al Sadr (whose spiritual mentor resides in Iran). Washington has also accused Iran of allowing foreign fighters to cross its borders into Iraq.

At the same time, Iranian leaders have taken advantage of the deteriorating security situation to intensify their condemnations of the U.S. presence in Iraq. This represents a combination of political opportunism and authentic empathy with the plight of the Iraqi people and the manifest instability in the sacred Shia shrine cities of Najaf and Karbala. No longer chastened by fears of Washington expanding its program of regime change, Iranian hard-liners are already asserting a newly reborn confidence that could easily tend toward greater audacity on the international scene. "The Americans, whether they want it or not, whether they accept it or not, are defeated in Iraq," Ayatollah Khamenei recently proclaimed.[4]

Notwithstanding these very real areas of conflict, there is considerable overlap between Iranian and U.S. visions for postwar Iraq. Although their strategic rationales vary widely, both Tehran and Washington are broadly committed to promoting a unitary and even pluralistic post-Saddam Iraqi state. For Iran, the driving forces are purely pragmatic; any partition of Iraq or outbreak of civil war could pose spillover effects, imperiling Iran's own stability. Although its hard-liners may maintain ties to the rabble-rousers such as al Sadr, they are unlikely to truly align themselves with his chaotic cause, or to champion the cause of Baathist remnants that terrorize

---

[4] "Iran Leader Pours Scorn on U.S. Democracy Claims," Reuters, June 3, 2004.

the Sunni center of the country. One Iranian newspaper derided the violence that has beset Iraq as neither guerrilla warfare nor the people's resistance, but rather "a horrible blind terror." Inconveniencing the United States is one thing; sowing turmoil in Iran's own environs is quite another. In fact, at the height of recent tensions in Najaf, Iran dispatched a team of diplomats to mediate between U.S. forces and the insurgent al Sadr forces.

Moreover, the Iranian clerics, who have resisted the expansion of popular political participation at home, are proving ardent champions of pluralism in Iraq. Again, this position, paradoxically, suits their interests—a democratic Iraqi polity is likely to feature strong Shia representation, providing Iran valuable avenues through which to exert its influence. In addition, such a state would be prone to internecine political squabbling and would thereby be an implausible rival for regional hegemony. For these reasons, the very clerics who undermined Iran's recent parliamentary polls have welcomed Iraq's new interim government and encouraged the early organization of free elections.

One of the central uncertainties about Iraq's evolution is the impact it may have on Iran's internal affairs. Many U.S. proponents of regime change suggested that Saddam Hussein's removal and the establishment of representative government and rule of law in Iraq would have a domino effect throughout the region, first and foremost in Iran. Undoubtedly, a stable, pluralistic Iraq that enjoys cordial relations with its neighbors may have ripple effects on the evolution of Iran's domestic political contention. And interaction between Iranian seminaries and the historic seats of religious scholarship in Iraq will intensify the debate among Shia clerics about the most appropriate relationship between religion and politics. Grand Ayatollah Ali Sistani commands a considerable following across the region—wider than that of any of Iran's ruling clergy. His quiet approach to clerical involvement in politics and his reported aversion to Iran's theocratic system could create new Iranian adherents to the notion of separating religion from politics. In the short term, however, instability in Iraq is only fueling the fires of extremism throughout the region.

Middle East Peace Process

Among the most troublesome practices of the Islamic Republic is its sustained and prolonged support for militant anti-Israeli groups and terrorists. Among these, Iran's sponsorship of Hezbollah remains the most significant. Iranian officials founded the group and continue to provide training, intelligence, arms, and financing twenty years later. An outgrowth of the intricate religious and familial ties among the region's Shia clerical establishment, Hezbollah today has both military and political arms but remains closely associated with Iran's clerical leadership.

Hezbollah's track record as one of the world's foremost terrorist organizations is indisputable: until 9/11, its 1983 attack on barracks housing U.S. Marines held the record for causing the largest loss of U.S. lives as a result of a terrorist attack. As a consequence of this attack and several other suicide bombings carried out by Hezbollah operatives during that period, Deputy Secretary of State Richard Armitage characterized the U.S. stance toward Hezbollah in late 2002 as a "blood debt." In the 1980s, Hezbollah was responsible for aircraft hijackings as well as kidnappings of U.S. citizens and other Westerners who were then held as hostages. In addition, Hezbollah operatives, along with four Iranian officials, have been indicted by Argentina in connection with the 1994 bombing of a Jewish community center that killed eighty-five people.

Despite this history, many within the region emphasize Hezbollah's political participation—its party members hold twelve seats in the Lebanese parliament—and openly supported its role in pressuring Israel to withdraw from southern Lebanon in 2000. In this regard, even U.S. allies are split to some extent. These reservations reflect Hezbollah's evolution into something beyond a compliant Iranian surrogate. Its organization and its history reflect the complicated rivalries within the Lebanese Shia community, as well as the formative role Syria has had in shaping the group's operational imperatives. Iranian material support, channeled via Damascus, remains significant, but reliable reports suggest that only a relatively small number of Iran's Revolutionary Guards remain in southern Lebanon today to help coordinate that assistance.

Iranian support for Hezbollah clearly transcends any factional differences among the Islamic Republic's political elite; both Iran's reformers and Iran's hard-liners are equally committed to the Lebanese organization. In fact, it is one of the leaders of the reformist faction of the 2000–2004 parliament—Hojjatoleslam Ali Akbar Mohtashamipur—who is credited with founding Hezbollah. President Khatami has met with its secretary general, Sheikh Hassan Nasrallah, several times in Lebanon and in Tehran, commenting recently that the group has a "a natural right, even a sacred national duty" to defend Palestinians against Israel.[5]

As a result, it is highly improbable that Iran can be persuaded or compelled to completely renounce its proxy. Still, some measure of Iranian flexibility may be possible even with respect to Hezbollah. Since 9/11, Iranian leaders have repeatedly advocated that Hezbollah exhibit restraint in its armed struggle against Israel, and have also hinted that a resolution to the Shebaa Farms territorial dispute could set the stage for Hezbollah to abandon its paramilitary activities.

Iran's long cultivation of Hezbollah, together with its extreme antagonism toward Israel, has paved the way for expanding relations with (Sunni) Palestinian militant groups, including the Popular Front for the Liberation of Palestine–General Command, Hamas, and Palestine Islamic Jihad. The connections among these groups, Hezbollah, and Iran have intensified steadily over the past fifteen years, as shared ideological views have facilitated operational linkages and alliances. Some reports estimate that Iran's support for individual organizations has been as high as $100 million, but Palestinian militants dispute these assertions, claiming that Iranian aid is philanthropic in nature and of

---

[5] Rob Synovitz, "Iran: Despite U.S. Pressure, Khatami Says Tehran Supports Hizballah," RFE/RL, May 14, 2003.

[34]

a much lesser magnitude. Tehran's support to these groups has complemented its long-standing antipathy toward Palestinian leader Yasir Arafat, whose Fatah movement aligned with Iraq during its war with Iran and who further alienated the Islamic Republic through his participation in the Madrid peace process that Tehran reviled.

Iran rejects U.S. criticism of its stance toward Israel and its support of Hezbollah and Palestinian militants; its official justifications differentiate between terrorist activities and what Tehran characterizes as legitimate resistance against occupation. This paradoxical position has generated occasional evidence that Iran could be persuaded to countenance an eventual peace agreement between the Palestinians and Israel. The foreign ministry declared, as recently as October 2002, that Iran would not stand in the way of a final two-state solution and accepted (at least in its official dialogue with Saudi Arabia) Crown Prince Abdullah's peace plan. Equally important, Iranian policymakers have recognized the risk that Iran's assistance to militants opposing the Middle East peace process could drag the country directly into conflict, particularly in the post-9/11 environment, where preemption is a tool of counterterrorism.

Still, the Iranian leadership's adherence to extremist rhetoric and its close association with rejectionist groups ultimately limits the government's flexibility on this issue. Having entrenched its opposition to Israel so prominently and absolutely, Tehran has found itself in the awkward position of being progressively more unyielding than the Palestinians themselves. Since the outset of the second Palestinian intifada in September 2000, the few official voices of moderation have been increasingly drowned out by radicalism. As a result, in spite of select and very modest improvements, Iran's involvement with terrorist groups and activities remains considerable according to U.S. and European intelligence. Most notably, in January 2002, a ship laden with fifty tons of Iranian weapons and explosives destined for the Palestinian Authority was discovered off the coast of Israel, with its captain claiming that its cargo was loaded in Iran. Iran has also continued to host an annual conclave on the intifada, which draws a veritable pantheon of terrorist leaders. As the U.S. war on terrorism begins to make headway against alternative sources of funding, these groups' reliance on Tehran may only be enhanced, which in turn would increase the incentives for Iranian hard-liners to seek low-cost proxies.

Although it is substantial, Iranian assistance does not constitute the primary factor in the existence or operations of Palestinian terrorism, however. Absent a return to discernible progress toward a peace settlement between Palestinians and Israelis and/or a meaningful commitment by the Palestinians to abandon violence against civilians as their primary means of confronting Israeli occupation, these groups and their abhorrent activities are likely to persist.

The Legacies of Iranian Support for Terrorism

It is important to highlight the fact that the international effort to curb Iran's terrorist associations has witnessed a few notable successes. Iran is credited with efforts to bring about the release of Western hostages held by Hezbollah in the early 1990s, for example, after rapprochement with the Gulf states dictated an abandonment of the proxy movements among their Shia populations. Furthermore, European efforts to prosecute Iranian officials for their involvement in extraterritorial assassinations of dissidents— notably, the German indictment of Iran's then intelligence minister in the 1997 "Mykonos case"—appears to have halted this once-prevalent practice. Most recently, Iranians internally have forced reforms (albeit very modest ones) of the intelligence ministry, the organization most closely identified with the practice of terrorism, as a result of popular outrage over the ministry's role in the 1998 murders of Iranian writers and political activists at home.

Unfortunately, each of these steps forward has occurred in the context of worrisome reversals on other issues. For example, the release of Western hostages in the early 1990s coincided with a renewed onslaught against Iranian dissidents abroad. The post-

9/11 dialogue with Washington on Afghanistan, meanwhile, took place even as support to militant Palestinian groups intensified and al-Qaeda operatives were found to have operated from Iranian territory. As a result of its tendency to subsume its foreign policy within its fierce domestic political competition, Iran has failed to achieve substantial diplomatic recompense for its limited bouts of cooperation.

As a result, the periods of progress in Iran's domestic political situation have not led to the sort of progress on the issue of terrorism that many once hoped for. Also complicating the situation is the fact that many Iranian reformers, although generally arguing for a less confrontational foreign policy, have also maintained steady ties with Lebanese and Palestinian militants, whose cause resonates with their own ideological roots in the Islamic left wing. Popular pressure is unlikely to prove a potent force for mitigating Iran's international adventurism, simply because of the extremely limited role of Iranian public opinion in shaping foreign policy. Thanks to the steady diet of propaganda, sympathy for the Palestinians' plight is more widely felt among Iranians today than prior to the revolution. Beyond a vocal minority, however, public sympathy does not extend to militancy, and anecdotal evidence suggests that Iranians are more concerned with expanding their own opportunities than those of a distant population.

Moreover, even if Iran's terrorist ties were fully severed today, their legacy would still be extremely problematic for the country. As a result of a 1996 U.S. law permitting lawsuits against state sponsors of terrorism, the Iranian government has been held liable for damages to families of Americans killed or wounded in terrorist bombings in Israel and kidnappings in Lebanon—damages that today total more than $1 billion. At the same time, criminal investigations into some of Iran's more far-flung alleged activities, such as the bombing of the Jewish community center in Argentina, have just begun to produce legal actions against former Iranian officials. Accountability and expectations of restitution will remain a serious dilemma for Iran if it is to move forward and one day fully reintegrate itself into the international community.

RECENT U.S. POLICY TOWARD TEHRAN

Formulating U.S. policy toward Tehran has never proved simple or straightforward. Enmeshed in its own contradictions and factional contestations, the Islamic Republic resists neat prognostication, and its leaders often act in ways that appear contrary to the country's interests.

In the twenty-five years that have passed since the 1979 revolution, Washington has deployed an array of policy tools, including sanctions, incentives, diplomacy, and military force. Since the mid-1990s, the United States has sought to contain the threat posed by Iran, relying increasingly on a set of economic sanctions that were at first comprehensive in scope but unilateral in application. These measures sought to alter Iran's objectionable policies by exacting considerable costs for such behavior and were coupled with a similar approach toward Iraq under the rubric of "dual containment." With respect to Tehran, the efficacy of this approach was undermined by Iran's concurrent efforts to rebuild its relations with its neighbors and major international actors, including Europe, China, and Japan.

In the late 1990s, the appearance of political liberalization in Iran persuaded the Clinton administration to discontinue the Iranian component of "dual containment." Although the bulk of the sanctions regime was maintained, Washington experimented with the possibility of engaging Tehran through modest unilateral gestures. The result was equally unsatisfying, producing only a frustrating exchange of missed opportunities as well as a continuation—and, in some important areas, an intensification—of the very Iranian policies that Washington sought to thwart. As with other aspects of his Middle East policy, President Clinton invested considerable personal attention with the intention of generating a breakthrough with Iran that might serve as a lasting legacy, only to find enhanced Iranian obstructionism as his reward.

The Bush administration had begun to outline a coherent policy toward Iran during its initial months in office—mobilizing a belated, and ultimately ineffective, effort to modify the

Iran-Libya Sanctions Act during its August 2001 reauthorization, for example—when the terrorist attacks of September 11, 2001, permanently altered its strategic calculus. In the post-9/11 environment, Iran appeared to embody the twin menaces now seen as the main threat facing the United States: terrorism and weapons of mass destruction. At the same time, with the initiation of Washington's war on terrorism, Iran became a key player in that effort, at least insofar as it involved Afghanistan and Iraq.

These dual imperatives helped to shape a disjointed and sometimes contradictory U.S. policy toward Tehran from late 2001 onward. The most dramatic development in U.S.-Iranian relations during this period was President Bush's decision to include Iran, along with Iraq and North Korea, in his construct of an "axis of evil" in his January 2002 State of the Union address. The reference came in response to the discovery of a weapons cache reportedly supplied by Iran en route to the Palestinian Authority, but it undercut several months of tacit cooperation between Washington and Tehran on the war and the post-conflict stabilization of Afghanistan.

At one end of the spectrum, the administration engaged Iran in a historic dialogue on Afghanistan, which was effective in generating greater Iranian cooperation (extraordinarily, the talks were publicly acknowledged within Iran). At the other end of the spectrum, some influential parties in Washington criticized the lack of democracy in Iran and appealed to Iranians for regime change in Tehran, renewing contacts with the same discredited expatriates who helped mastermind the Iran-Contra debacle in the 1980s. Differing views in Washington generated occasionally glaring inconsistencies in U.S. positions. In the aftermath of the ouster of Saddam Hussein, for example, the Pentagon publicly flirted with utilizing an Iraq-based Iranian opposition group as a vanguard force against Tehran over the protests of the State Department, which had designated the group as a foreign terrorist organization in 1997.

The U.S. war on terrorism has complicated the process of dealing with a country such as Iran, which is experiencing internal pressures and a slow evolution away from radicalism, and whose politics and predilections are ambiguous and opaque. Flawed assumptions about Iran's murky internal situation have weakened the effectiveness of U.S. policy toward the country in recent years. Persuaded that revolutionary change was imminent in Iran, the administration sought to influence Iran's internal order, relying on the model of the east European transition from communism. However, the neat totalitarian dichotomy between the regime and the people does not exist in the Islamic Republic, and, as a result, frequent, vocal appeals to the "Iranian people" only strengthened the cause of clerical reactionaries and left regime opponents vulnerable to charges of being Washington's "fifth column."

ASSESSMENTS AND RECOMMENDATIONS

The United States' long lack of direct contact with, and presence in, Iran drastically impedes its understanding of Iran's domestic, as well as regional, dynamics. In turn, this reduces Washington's influence across the Middle East in ways that are manifestly harmful to its ultimate interests. Direct dialogue approached candidly and without restrictions on issues of mutual concern would serve Iran's interests. And establishing connections with Iranian society would directly benefit U.S. national objectives of enhancing the stability and security of this critical region.

Dialogue between the United States and Iran need not await absolute harmony between the two governments. Throughout history, Washington has maintained cordial and constructive relations with regimes whose policies and philosophies have differed significantly from its own, including, above all, in its relationship with the Soviet Union. By its very definition, diplomacy seeks to address issues between nations, and so it would be unwise (and unrealistic) to defer contact with Tehran until all differences between the two governments have evaporated.

Conversely, however, any significant expansion in the U.S. relationship with Tehran must incorporate unimpeachable progress toward a satisfactory resolution of key U.S. concerns. Political and economic relations with Iran cannot be normalized unless and until the Iranian government demonstrates a commitment to abandoning its nuclear weapons programs and its support for terrorist groups. However, these demands should not constitute preconditions for dialogue.

In launching any new relationship with Iran, it is important that expectations on both sides are realistic and that U.S. ones are clearly communicated to the Iranians as well as between the various players in the U.S. foreign policy bureaucracy. A "grand bargain" between Iran and the United States is not a realistic or achievable goal. A quarter century of enmity and estrangement are not easily overcome, the issues at stake are too numerous and complex, and the domestic political contexts of both countries are too difficult to allow the current breach to be settled comprehensively overnight. Moreover, even the most far-reaching rapprochement between the United States and Iran could not re-create the close alliance that existed prior to the revolution in 1979. Were the most serious U.S. concerns about Iranian behavior to be resolved, significant differences between worldviews and strategic priorities would remain. Instead, we envision a relationship through which the two countries pragmatically explore areas of common concern and potential cooperation, while continuing to pursue other incompatible objectives at the same time.

For these reasons, we advocate that Washington propose a compartmentalized process of dialogue, confidence building, and incremental engagement. The United States should identify the discrete set of issues on which critical U.S. and Iranian interests converge and must be prepared to try to make progress along separate tracks, even while considerable differences remain in other areas.

Instead of aspiring to a detailed road map of rapprochement, as previous U.S. administrations have recommended, the executive branch should consider outlining a more simple mechanism for framing formal dialogue with Iran. A basic statement of principles, along the lines of the 1972 Shanghai Communiqué signed by the United States and China, could be developed to outline the parameters for U.S.-Iranian engagement, establish the overarching objectives for dialogue, and reassure relevant domestic political constituencies on both sides. The effort to draft such a statement would give constructive focus and substance to a serious but realistic bilateral dialogue. Should that effort reach stalemate, dialogue should still move forward on specific issues.

In engaging with Iran, the United States must be prepared to utilize incentives as well as punitive measures. Given Iran's pressing economic challenges, the most powerful inducements for Tehran would be economic measures: particularly steps that rescind the comprehensive U.S. embargo on trade and investment in Iran. Used judiciously, such incentives could enhance U.S. leverage vis-à-vis Tehran. One particularly valuable step, which should be made conditional on significant progress in resolving one or more of the chief concerns with respect to Iran, would be the authorization of executory contracts—legal instruments that permit U.S. businesses to negotiate with Iranian entities but defer ultimate implementation of any agreements until further political progress has been reached. Commercial relations represent a diplomatic tool that should not be underestimated or cynically disregarded. Ultimately, the return of U.S. businesses to Tehran could help undermine the clerics' monopoly on power by strengthening the nonstate sector, improving the plight of Iran's beleaguered middle class, and offering new opportunities to transmit American values.

In dealing with Iran, the United States should relinquish the rhetoric of regime change. Such language inevitably evokes the problematic history of U.S. involvement with the 1953 coup that unseated Iranian Prime Minister Mohammad Mossadeq. For these reasons, propounding regime change simply invites nationalist passions that are clearly unconstructive to the cause such a policy would seek to serve. Rather, Washington's positions and policies must clearly communicate to the government and citizens of Iran that the United States favors political evolution: the long-range vision is an Iran that ushers in democracy itself in a meaningful and lasting manner.

Nuclear Programs

Iran's history of maintaining clandestine programs suggests that a radical change in its strategic environment would be the only enduring way its nuclear weapons programs could be thwarted. In dealing with a state determined to maintain a nuclear option, counterproliferation efforts can only succeed in escalating the time and cost associated with such programs. A permanent solution must address the catalyst that drives Iran's pursuit of nuclear weapons: its persistent sense of insecurity vis-à-vis both regional rivals and its paramount adversary, the United States. Ultimately, only in the context of an overall rapprochement with Washington will there be any prospect of persuading Iran to make the strategic decision to relinquish its nuclear program.

Short of such a fundamental breakthrough in Iran's own stance, the International Atomic Energy Agency process offers a viable path for managing Iran's nuclear efforts, provided that there is close multilateral coordination and firm U.S. leadership. A strong European role is essential in marshalling an effective combination of pressure and incentives. But there must be direct U.S. engagement in the process to maintain vigilance and persuade Tehran of the potential costs of noncompliance. The United States should intensify its engagement with its allies on this issue. Although enhanced international scrutiny of Iran's weapons programs cannot permanently neutralize Iran's nuclear aspirations, the IAEA can play an active role in retarding these programs and in generating a coordinated multilateral stance. To this end, the United States should continue to press the agency to enforce the Nonproliferation Treaty's Additional Protocol and pursue snap comprehensive inspections of Iranian facilities. Iran will provide an important test case for this verification instrument. In addition, the United States should work with the Europeans and with the IAEA to identify a set of "red lines"—conditions that, if Iran failed to fulfill, would trigger a referral of Iran's case to the United Nations Security Council. Tehran must clearly understand that unless it demonstrates real, uninterrupted cooperation with the IAEA process, it will face the prospect of multilateral sanctions imposed by the Security Council.

Further, the Task Force recommends that the United States work with its allies and the IAEA to outline a detailed framework agreement that would seek to outline a more durable solution to the nuclear issue. The basic parameters of such an agreement would institute ongoing rigorous constraints on Iran's nuclear program in exchange for continued access to peaceful technology and international markets. Iran would be asked to commit to permanently ceasing all its enrichment and reprocessing activities, subject to international verification. In return, the international community would guarantee access to adequate nuclear fuel supplies, with assurances that all spent fuel would be returned to the country of origin, and to advanced power generation technology (whose export to Iran is currently restricted). These commitments would permit the continuing development of a peaceful Iranian nuclear power program and provide multilateral guarantees of access to nuclear technology, as long as Iran abides by its nonproliferation obligations defined broadly to include cessation of uranium enrichment.

Iran will inevitably resist such a proposal, as it has vocally proclaimed its sovereign rights to nuclear technology and to all those activities not specifically prohibited by the Nonproliferation Treaty. For this reason, the framework agreement should incorporate a new combination of carrots and sticks to persuade Tehran to reconsider its course. In particular, the United States should be prepared to commit to opening a bilateral dialogue with Iran on enhancing political and economic relations that would take place in parallel with the Islamic Republic's established negotiations with the European Union on trade, terrorism, proliferation, the Middle East peace process, and human rights.

A viable framework agreement with Iran on the nuclear issue would demand more effective cooperation between Washington and its allies to make clear to Iran both the potential rewards for its cooperation as well as the possible costs of its continuing obstructionism. Although the United States must take a leader-ship role, the involvement of its allies and multilateral institutions will be essential to provide leverage vis-à-vis Iran. The United States should carefully calibrate any approach to garner the widest con-sensus and a firm commitment to a coordinated set of steps. For example, the United States should focus its dialogue with Russia not on pressuring Moscow to abandon its involvement with the construction of the Bushehr nuclear power plant, but on persuading it to intensify its efforts to reach an agreement on the return of spent fuel from that facility. For its part, the European Union must be willing to consider curtailing economic relations with Tehran should Iran be unwilling to adopt greater controls on its nuclear programs.

Given the potential threat that Iran's acquisition of nuclear weapons could pose, the full range of alternatives—including military options—for confronting Tehran must be examined. Yet the use of military force would be extremely problematic, given the dis-persal of Iran's program at sites throughout the country and their proximity to urban centers. Since Washington would be blamed for any unilateral Israeli military strike, the United States should make it quite clear to Israel that U.S. interests would be adverse-ly affected by such a move. In addition, any military effort to elim-inate Iranian weapons capabilities would run the significant risk of reinforcing Tehran's desire to acquire a nuclear deterrent and of provoking nationalist passions in defense of that very course. It would most likely also generate hostile Iranian initiatives in Iraq and Afghanistan.

Regional Conflicts

From the perspective of U.S. interests, one particular issue area appears particularly ripe for U.S.-Iranian engagement: the future of Iraq and Afghanistan. The United States has a direct and compelling interest in ensuring both countries' security and the success of their post-conflict governments. Iran has demonstrated its ability and readiness to use its influence constructively in these two countries, but also its capacity for making trouble. The United States should work with Tehran to capitalize on Iran's influence to advance the stability and consolidation of its neighbors. This could commence via a resumption and expansion of the Geneva track discussions with Tehran on post-conflict Afghanistan and Iraq.

Such a dialogue should be structured to obtain constructive Iranian involvement in the process of consolidating authority within the central governments and rebuilding the economies of both Iraq and Afghanistan. Regular contact with Iran would also provide a channel to address concerns that have arisen about its activities and relationships with competing power centers in both countries. These discussions should incorporate other regional power brokers, as well as Europe and Russia—much like the "Six Plus Two" negotiations on Afghanistan that took place in the years before the Taliban were ousted. A multilateral forum on the future of Iraq and Afghanistan would help cultivate confidence and would build political and economic relationships essential to the long-term durability of the new governments in Baghdad and Kabul.

Critics have argued that Iran should be denied any formal role in the reconstruction of Iraq due to the propensity of some Iranian factions to pursue destabilizing policies there. In the aftermath of the June 28, 2004, handover of sovereignty to the interim Iraqi administration, however, the United States is no longer in a position to implement such a veto, nor should it endeavor to do so. Convincing Iran that it has a direct stake in the successful transition of its former adversary represents the most effective means of thwarting any attempts by hard-line elements in Iran to undermine Iraq.

Over the longer term, U.S. interests in achieving peace and stability in the Persian Gulf would be best served by engaging Iran and each of its neighbors in a dialogue aimed at establishing an effective organization to promote regional security and cooperation. Such an organization could be structured to provide a forum for regional dialogue, confidence-building measures, economic cooperation, conflict prevention, and crisis management.

Settling the al-Qaeda issue must remain a high priority for the United States. Through direct dialogue with Afghanistan via a renewed Geneva track, the outlines of a reciprocal arrangement should be negotiated. In private discussions, the Iranian government has already suggested the outlines of an agreement that would trade al-Qaeda detainees for members of an Iraqi-based opposition group, the Mojahideen-e Khalq, which has long perpetrated terrorist activities against Iran. Such an explicit trade is not possible, however, due to the impossibility of ensuring fair adjudication in the Iranian system. Rather, the Task Force recommends that the United States press Iran to clarify the status of all al-Qaeda–related detainees and to extradite those who can be identified as persons pursued by other governments. At the same time, the United States should work with the interim Iraqi government to ensure that Mojahideen facilities are conclusively disbanded and that its leaders are brought to justice for their role in violence against both Iraqis and Iranians under Saddam's regime.

Iran's involvement in the Israeli-Palestinian conflict is a pernicious factor in an already debilitating conflict. Ultimately, the most effective strategy for extracting Iran from the Israeli-Palestinian conflict would be resuming a robust peace process buttressed by a sustained U.S. commitment to lead the effort and a broad regional consensus in support of the negotiating parties and the ultimate agreements. Should leading Arab states such as Saudi Arabia and Egypt actively support and facilitate a peace process between Israelis and Palestinians, Iran would be likely to acquiesce to this process. Iranian hostility toward the peace process is not immutable— a lonely struggle against an emerging regional consensus on behalf of radical Palestinian forces is not likely to be the path chosen by Tehran.

Long-Term Relations with Iran

Washington should work to ensure that its rhetoric and policies target Iran's objectionable policies rather than its population. Attempting to isolate the Iranian people does not serve the cause of democracy in Iran or the region. The most appropriate and effective mechanism for contributing to Iran's slow process of change would be to intensify the political, cultural, and economic linkages between its population and the wider world. Specifically, this should entail gradually incorporating Iran into the activities of the U.S. Middle East Partnership Initiative and other regional reform programs and issuing a blanket license to authorize the activities of U.S. nongovernmental organizations in Iran. The administration should also take care to ensure that its message—that the United States desires a dialogue on mutual interests and that the resumption of relations will require a positive response from Iran regarding U.S. concerns—is crystal clear to both the government and the people of Iran.

Successive U.S. administrations have centered their policy toward Iran on the persuasive power of economic sanctions to change the country's positions and conduct. The comprehensive and unilateral nature of the U.S. embargo, however, ultimately deprives Washington of leverage: both the influence that comes with a government's ability to make trade ties conditional on improved political relations and the more diffuse impact business relations can have on changing political culture. The Task Force ultimately concludes that economic relations between the United States and Iran must be conditioned upon improvements in the diplomatic relationship between the two countries. Small steps, such as the authorization of trade between U.S. entities and Iran's relatively small private sector, should be contemplated as confidence-building measures that would create new constituencies within Iran for a government that is fully integrated into the international community. In addition, the United States should relinquish its efforts to prevent Iranian engagement with international financial institutions, as these efforts are inherently counterproductive to the objective of promoting better governance in Tehran. Permitting Iran to begin accession talks with the World Trade Organization will only intensify pressure on Tehran for accountability and transparency, and may help facilitate Iran's evolution into a state that respects its citizens and its neighbors.

ADDITIONAL AND DISSENTING VIEWS

I wish to stress that support for dialogue and diplomatic and economic relations between Iran and the United States does not imply acquiescence in the violation by the Iranian government of the civil rights and liberties of its own citizens. Some Iranians understandably fear that relations with the United States will reinforce the status quo and therefore regime durability in Iran. In fact, any study of Iranian history over the last century and more suggests that interaction with the outside world greatly accelerates, rather than hinders, the pace of internal political change. I believe enmeshing Iran with the international community, expanding trade, and improving economic opportunity and the conditions for the growth of the middle class will strengthen, not weaken, the democratic forces in Iran.

Shaul Bakhash

While I agree with the main thrust of the report I do not agree that the U.S. interventions in Iraq and Afghanistan may offer Iran new incentives to open a mutually beneficial dialogue. On the contrary, I believe Iran has few incentives for dialogue. They are convinced we intend to overthrow them, and they believe we are bogged down in Iraq and have lost what support we had in the Arab world. From their perspective, it is better to wait and let us stew in our own juice. Overtures on our part, under these circumstances, are likely to be interpreted as a sign of weakness and be rebuffed.

Frank Carlucci

The Task Force report offers sound and insightful analysis of the evolution of the Islamic Republic's internal politics, its foreign policy, and the range of U.S. interests at stake in America's relationship with Iran. However, I must take exception with the report's conclusion that a "grand bargain" between the United States and Iran is not a realistic goal. Indeed, I believe that a grand bargain may be the only realistic option for breaking out of the current impasse in U.S.-Iranian relations, which is increasingly dysfunctional for U.S. interests.

We have had considerable experience, over the years, with incremental or issue-specific approaches to seeking an improved U.S.-Iranian relationship. In Lebanon, Bosnia, and, most recently, in Afghanistan, U.S.-Iranian cooperation has been important to the achievement of U.S. policy goals in challenging environments. Yet, this cooperation has never been able to serve as the catalyst for more fundamental and strategic improvement in the U.S.-Iranian relationship. Disagreements over other critical issues—especially terrorism and nonproliferation—have always undermined the strategic potential of U.S.-Iranian tactical cooperation. I see no reason, in the current climate, to believe that the kind of approach recommended in the report is more likely to succeed in improving the overall nature of the U.S.-Iranian relationship than earlier exercises in incremental, issue-specific cooperation.

I have assumed for some years that the biggest problem the United States faces in trying to get the Iranian government to change its approach toward proliferation and support for terrorism is that most Iranian citizens have heretofore had no clear reason to "connect the dots" between their government's ending its support both for Hezbollah and for nuclear weapons development and having U.S. economic sanctions lifted as a result. If such a connection were made, you might find the majority of Iranians demanding good behavior by their government on these issues because the vast majority wants a better relationship with the United States, as they believe that a normalized relationship with the United States is in their own economic and social self-interest.

Finally, the United States should make certain that the Iranian people clearly "hear" this offer of a grand bargain. We should make this offer to the Iranian government (I would suggest through Hassan Rohani, secretary general of Iran's Supreme National Security Council), but also broadcast it directly to the Iranian people. I believe the "conservatives" in Iran will also see such an approach as a chance for them to undertake a "Nixon to China" approach and, potentially achieve a goal that has benefits both internationally and, more important, domestically as they attempt to cement their political position long term.

H. P. Goldfield

In consideration of the Senate Select Committee on Intelligence's report of July 7, 2004, on Iraq and 9/11, I believe the Council on Foreign Relations Task Force report on Iran should be very circumspect on what it concludes is happening in Iran. Until such time as U.S. intelligence is confirmed reliable, or Americans can be assured the administration has not distorted the intelligence it receives, the report should be very cautious on what it recommends based on the assumption its intelligence is correct.

Furthermore, I would have preferred that the final report dealt with engagement, beginning with subjects of common interest to the United States and Iran, rather than suggesting that engagement selectively deal only with well-known but unconfirmed contentious subjects. It is certain Iran would have its own list of similar issues that the United States perceived to threaten its security. This is not a starting point for effective engagement.

In a relative sense, in the region, I do not agree that Iran is an unstable country. In fact, it well may be the most stable. Although not quantified, it appears that those who have long been supported most aggressively by the United States have a much higher potential for instability than does Iran.

The report's conclusion that isolation, containment sanctions, and the like have failed as foreign policy practices by the United States is welcomed. And the conclusion that the United States should adopt measures to broaden political, cultural, and economic linkages with the people of Iran is even more welcomed.

Richard H. Matzke

———————————

The report proposes a framework agreement under which Iran would cease permanently all enrichment and reprocessing activities under international verification, in exchange for guaranteed access to nuclear fuel and assured return of spent fuel to the country of origin. Russia could play a central role in advancing this kind of approach, having enacted legislation permitting it to import spent fuel from other countries, with a view to generating substantial revenues from reactor operators in countries seeking a way to facilitate the difficult task of managing growing stocks of spent fuel. It would be in the interest of the United States to engage Russia in early discussions to negotiate an agreement of peaceful nuclear cooperation that would permit Russia to import spent fuel of U.S. origin, to reinforce U.S. efforts to persuade Moscow to conclude and implement its proposed agreement with Iran for the return to Russia of the spent fuel from the Bushehr nuclear reactor. It is worth noting that the nonproliferation benefits of this kind of approach—essentially providing cradle-to-grave fuel services to countries that forswear dangerous fuel-cycle activities—could extend well beyond Iran.

Also, the report properly notes that Iran is permitted to enrich uranium and engage in other nuclear fuel-cycle facilities under its international treaty obligations, but it should be remembered that, according to Article IV of the Nuclear Nonproliferation Treaty, the grant of the inalienable right to develop nuclear energy is qualified by the phrase "for peaceful purposes." Thus if the international community should conclude that Iranian efforts to enrich uranium or obtain plutonium were intended, in fact, to support the development of nuclear weapons, then those Iranian efforts would not be permissible under its international treaty obligations.

Daniel B. Poneman

TASK FORCE MEMBERS

PETER ACKERMAN is Managing Director of Rockport Capital and Chairman of the Board Overseers of the Fletcher School of Law and Diplomacy. He is the co-author of *A Force More Powerful: A Century of Nonviolent Conflict* and Executive Producer of "Bringing Down a Dictator," the Peabody Award–winning documentary on the fall of Slobodan Milosevic.

DAVID ALBRIGHT is President and founder of the Institute for Science and International Security. He is a physicist who specializes in nuclear nonproliferation. For over a decade he has assessed and published widely on Iran's secret nuclear efforts. In the 1990s, he worked with the IAEA Action Team mandated by the UN Security Council to dismantle and monitor against any reconstitution of Iraq's nuclear weapons programs.

SHAUL BAKHASH* is Clarence J. Robinson Professor of History at George Mason University. He is the author of *Iran: Monarchy, Bureaucracy and Reform under the Oajars, 1858–1896; The Politics of Oil and Revolution in Iran;* and *Reign of the Ayatollahs: Iran and the Islamic Revolution.* His articles have appeared in the *New York Review of Books,* the *New Republic, Foreign Policy,* the *Journal of Democracy,* and in scholarly books and journals. He has written opinion pieces for the *New York Times,* the *Washington Post,* the *LA Times,* and other newspapers. He worked for many years as a journalist in Iran, writing for the Tehran-based *Kayhan Newspapers* as well as for the *London Times,* the *Financial Times,* and the *Economist.* Before coming to

---

Note: Task Force members participate in their individual and not institutional capacities.

* The individual has endorsed the report and submitted an additional or a dissenting view.

George Mason University in 1985, he taught at Princeton University. He spent the past year as a Visiting Fellow at the Saban Center at the Brookings Institution, working on a book on the reform movement in Iran.

ZBIGNIEW BRZEZINSKI is Co-Chair of the Task Force and served as National Security Adviser to President Carter from 1977 to 1981. He is the author of, most recently, *The Choice: Global Domination or Global Leadership.*

FRANK CARLUCCI* is Chairman Emeritus of the Carlyle Group, having served as Chairman for eleven years. His government background includes service as Secretary of Defense, National Security Adviser, Deputy Director of Central Intelligence, Ambassador, Deputy Director of OMB, and Undersecretary of Health, Education, and Welfare.

ROBERT EINHORN is Senior Adviser at the Center for Strategic and International Studies and served as Assistant Secretary of State for Nonproliferation from 1999 to August 2001.

ROBERT M. GATES is Co-Chair of the Task Force and President of Texas A&M University. Dr. Gates served as Director of Central Intelligence from 1991 to 1993. In this position, he headed all foreign intelligence agencies of the United States and directed the Central Intelligence Agency. Dr. Gates has been awarded the National Security Medal and the Presidential Citizens Medal, has twice received the National Intelligence Distinguished Service Medal, and has three times received the CIA's highest award, the Distinguished Intelligence Medal.

H. P. GOLDFIELD* is Vice Chairman of Stonebridge International, LLC, an international strategic advisory firm based in Washington, DC, and a Senior International Adviser to the law firm of Hogan & Hartson LLP. Previously, Mr. Goldfield served as Assistant Secretary of Commerce for Trade Development and as Associate Counsel to President Ronald Reagan. Mr. Goldfield also serves on the Boards of Directors of Black & Veatch Holding Company, the Middle East Institute, and the Israel Policy Forum.

STEPHEN B. HEINTZ is President of the Rockefeller Brothers Fund. Prior to joining RBF, he was founding President of Demos, a public policy research and advocacy network. After fifteen years in public service, he served as Executive Vice President of the EastWest Institute, based in Prague, from 1990 to 1997.

BRUCE HOFFMAN is Director of the RAND Corporation's Washington Office and Acting Director of RAND's Center for Middle East Public Policy. He is also a Senior Fellow at the Combating Terrorism Center at the U.S. Military Academy, in West Point, NY.

JOHN H. KELLY was Assistant Secretary of State for the Near East and South Asia from 1989 to 1991, Ambassador to Lebanon from 1986 to 1988, and Ambassador to Finland from 1991 to 1994. Since then, he has been an international consultant and Ambassador-in-Residence at the Sam Nunn School of International Affairs, at Georgia Tech.

WILLIAM H. LUERS is President of the United Nations Association of USA and served as an American diplomat for thirty years, including serving as Ambassador to Venezuela and Czechoslovakia. He subsequently served as President of the Metropolitan Museum of Art for thirteen years. In his current position, which he has held for five years, he has been involved in high-level discussions on U.S. policy toward Iran.

SUZANNE MALONEY, Director of this Task Force, has served as Middle East adviser for a major international oil company and as Olin

---

* The individual has endorsed the report and submitted an additional or a dissenting view.

Fellow at the Brookings Institution. She is the author of a forthcoming book, *Ayatollah Gorbachev: The Politics of Change in Khatami's Iran.*

RICHARD H. MATZKE* is President of NESW Solutions; a member of the Board of Directors of OAO LUKoil, Russia's largest oil company; former Vice Chairman of the Chevron Texaco Corporation; and Co-Chairman of the American Iranian Council.

LOUIS PERLMUTTER has been an investment banker and has participated in various second-track diplomatic discussions over the past twenty years.

JAMES PLACKE served much of his twenty-seven-year Foreign Service career in Middle East oil-exporting countries, concluding as a Deputy Assistant Secretary of State for Near Eastern Affairs, with responsibility for Iran, Iraq, and the Gulf states, and for U.S. economic relations with the Arab region. He has since been a consultant on Middle East energy economics and strategy affiliated with Cambridge Energy Research Associates.

NICHOLAS PLATT is President Emeritus of the Asia Society. He served as Ambassador to Pakistan, the Philippines, and Zambia in the course of a thirty-four-year Foreign Service career. The Asia Society organized Iran-related policy programs, cultural events, and in-country travel during his tenure as President.

DANIEL B. PONEMAN,* former Special Assistant to the President for Nonproliferation and Export Controls, served on the National Security Council staff under Presidents George H. W. Bush and Bill Clinton. A Senior Fellow at the Forum for International Policy, he is co-author of *Going Critical: The First North Korean Nuclear Crisis.*

ELAHÉ SHARIFPOUR-HICKS is an independent human rights activist. She spent ten years working as the Iran researcher for Human Rights Watch. She has also worked for the United Nations Office of the High Commissioner for Human Rights and for Human Rights First. Sharifpour-Hicks has traveled repeatedly to Iran on human rights missions. She is a frequent commentator on human rights and related policy issues on the Farsi services of the BBC, VOA, RFI, and RFE. She is a graduate of Tehran University Faculty of Law and Political Science. She received her LLM in international law at Fordham Law School in New York.

STEPHEN J. SOLARZ served in public office for twenty-four years, both in the New York State Assembly and in the U.S. House of Representatives. Mr. Solarz served for eighteen years on the U.S. House of Representatives International Affairs Committee, emerging as a leading spokesman on behalf of democracy and human rights. He co-authored the resolution authorizing the use of force in the first Persian Gulf War and led the successful fight for its passage on the House floor.

RAY TAKEYH is a Professor of National Security Studies at the National Defense University.

MORTIMER ZUCKERMAN is Editor-in-Chief of *U.S. News & World Report* and Publisher of New York's *Daily News* and served as a Middle East adviser to President Bill Clinton.

---

* The individual has endorsed the report and submitted an additional or a dissenting view.

TASK FORCE OBSERVERS

RACHEL BRONSON
Council on Foreign Relations

STEVEN A. COOK
Council on Foreign Relations

RYAN C. CROCKER
National Defense University

LEE FEINSTEIN
Council on Foreign Relations

JUDITH KIPPER
Council on Foreign Relations

DAVID L. PHILLIPS
Council on Foreign Relations

KIM SAVIT
Senate Committee on Foreign Relations

PUNEET TALWAR
Senate Committee on Foreign Relations

APPENDIXES

Appendix A

Important Dates in U.S.-Iranian History

January 16, 1979	Shah Mohammad Reza Pahlavi flees Iran on the heels of mass demonstrations and strikes.
February 1, 1979	Ayatollah Khomeini returns from exile.
November 4, 1979	Iranian students seize 63 hostages at the U.S. embassy in Tehran.
April 25, 1980	A secret U.S. military mission to rescue hostages ends in disaster in a sandstorm in a central Iranian desert.
July 27, 1980	Exiled shah dies of cancer in Egypt.
September 22, 1980	Iraq declares war against Iran.
January 20, 1981	As President Ronald Reagan is inaugurated, Iran releases the remaining 52 American hostages after 444 days of detention.
January 20, 1984	The United States declares Iran a sponsor of international terrorism, making Iran ineligible for various forms of U.S. foreign assistance.
1985–86	Washington and Tehran engage in a complex scheme to fund assistance to Nicaraguan rebels through proceeds of U.S. weapons sales to Iran.
August 1986	The United States prohibits Iran from receiving U.S. arms (including spare parts) under the U.S. Arms Export Control Act.
1987–88	Hostilities between Tehran and Baghdad draw in neighbors and international shippers. The United States and Iran engage in open and direct conflict in the "tanker war."

October 29, 1987	President Reagan signs Executive Order 12613, which bans U.S. imports of Iranian crude oil and all other Iranian imports because of Iran's support for terrorism and its threat to maritime traffic in the Persian Gulf.
July 3, 1988	USS *Vincennes* mistakenly shoots down an Iran Air Airbus over the Persian Gulf, killing all 290 people on board.
July 20, 1988	Iran formally accepts UN Resolution 598, calling for a cease-fire between Iran and Iraq, ending its war with Iraq.
January 20, 1989	In his inaugural speech, President George H. W. Bush refers to U.S. hostages in Lebanon and adds (in what was interpreted as an overture to Iran), "Assistance can be shown here, and will be long remembered. Good will begets good will."
June 3, 1989	Ayatollah Khomeini dies. Hojjatoleslam Ali Khamenei, who has served two terms as president, is appointed supreme leader. Two months later, Hashemi Rafsanjani is sworn in as Iran's president.
1990–91	Iran remains neutral in U.S.-led Operation Desert Storm.
October 1992	Iran-Iraq Arms Nonproliferation Act is signed into law.
March 5, 1995	U.S. oil company Conoco signs a $1 billion deal to develop Iranian oil fields, the first such contract since the 1979 revolution; Conoco subsequently backs out of the deal after strenuous objections in Washington.
March 15, 1995	President Bill Clinton issues Executive Order 12957, banning U.S. investment in Iran's energy sector.
May 6, 1995	President Clinton issues Executive Order 12959, banning U.S. trade and investment in Iran.

August 4, 1996	President Clinton signs the Iran-Libya Sanctions Act (ILSA) into law, which imposes at least two out of a menu of six sanctions on foreign companies that make an "investment" of more than $20 million in one year in Iran's energy sector.
November 22, 1996	The European Union adopts "blocking legislation" to prevent European companies from complying with ILSA.
May 23, 1997	Hojjatoleslam Mohammad Khatami wins Iran's presidential election.
October 9, 1997	The U.S. State Department announces that the Mojahideen-e Khalq Organization (MKO) has been designated a foreign terrorist organization, banning fund-raising for it in the United States.
January 8, 1998	President Khatami calls for a "dialogue with the American people" in a CNN interview.
June 17, 1998	U.S. Secretary of State Madeleine Albright gives a major policy address on Iran, proposing the two countries construct a "road map" for better relations.
July 31, 1998	Former hostage Barry Rosen meets with former student militant Abbas Abdi.
September 16, 1998	Two hundred and twenty congressmen sign a letter condemning Iran and calling for U.S. support for the outlawed opposition group MKO.
September 21, 1998	President Khatami address the UN General Assembly; Foreign Minister Kamal Kharrazi backs out of Afghan meeting where he was to have met Albright.
November 5, 1998	The U.S. government rejects an application from a Texas firm for oil swaps between Iran and Kazakhstan.

January 13, 1999	The U.S. government sanctions three Russian institutes for cooperating with Iran.
April 28, 1999	The Clinton administration loosens sanctions to permit sales of food and medicine to Iran.
July 1, 1999	One hundred and thirty congressmen sign a letter criticizing the Iranian regime and advocating support of MKO. A pro-MKO rally in Washington draws the participation of several members of Congress.
July 1999	Major protests erupt in Tehran and many other Iranian cities; the United States criticizes the repression of student demonstrators.
November 22, 1999	The State Department confirms that Iran rejected a U.S. request to permit consular visits.
December 3, 1999	The U.S. government authorizes sales of Boeing spare parts to Iran.
February 18, 2000	Iranian reformists win a landslide victory in a general election.
February 24, 2000	The U.S. Senate unanimously approves the Iran Nonproliferation Act; the House passes it with unanimous support one week later.
March 17, 2000	Secretary of State Albright calls for a new start in U.S.-Iranian relations and announces the lifting of sanctions on caviar, carpets, and pistachios.
March 24, 2000	Former Lebanon hostage Terry Anderson wins a lawsuit against Iran by default; Tehran is found liable for $341 million in damages.
April 14, 2000	The United States announces sanctions on four Iranian entities, including the Defense Ministry, for missile proliferation.
June 4, 2000	President Khatami's adviser on women's issues attends a UN conference in New

York; several in the delegation return to Iran to protest having been fingerprinted.

July 4, 2000 · Iran protests the U.S. fingerprinting policy by blocking the U.S. soccer team from visiting to play a scheduled match.

July 10, 2000 · Nine thousand people protest an espionage conviction for Iranian Jews in front of Iran's UN Mission; the U.S. ambassador to the United Nations, Richard Holbrooke, attends.

August 31, 2000 · Karrubi and other Iranian MPs visit New York for an international parliamentary session and meet several U.S. congressmen at a reception. At the same time, several State Department officials visit Iran to participate in a UN conference.

September 6–7, 2000 · President Clinton and Secretary of State Albright attend President Khatami's speeches to the UN General Assembly in New York.

September 15, 2000 · Secretary of State Albright and the Iranian foreign minister participate in a joint UN session on Afghanistan.

May 4, 2001 · The Iranian wrestling team visits the United States for World Cup matches.

June 21, 2001 · The United States issues indictments in the 1996 Khobar Towers bombing, implicating Iran as having directed the attack by a little-known group of Saudi Shia.

August 3, 2001 · President George W. Bush signs the ILSA Extension Act into law.

September 2001 · After the 9/11 attacks, Friday prayers in Tehran omit "Death to America" chants for the first time in recent history; sermons condemn the terror attacks; Tehran's mayor sends a condolence letter to New York's mayor; several hundred Iranians gather for a candlelight vigil, but security forces break up the event.

October 9, 2001 President Khatami calls for an "immediate end" to U.S. military strikes on the Taliban; the following day, more than 150 MPs vote to condemn the U.S. bombing of Afghanistan.

October 10, 2001 The United States blocks Iran's bid to begin accession talks with the World Trade Organization (WTO).

October 17, 2001 Iran's UN ambassador visits Washington for a dinner with U.S. congressmen. The United States announces that Iran has promised to rescue any U.S. pilots shot down over Iran (the agreement came in letters exchanged at the start of the Afghanistan conflict, on October 7).

November 12, 2001 The Iranian Foreign Minister and U.S. Secretary of State Colin Powell meet at an international session on Afghanistan and shake hands in an unprecedented diplomatic overture.

January 3, 2002 Israeli forces seize a Palestinian freight ship loaded with fifty tons of arms; both Israel and the United States charge Iran with masterminding the operation and sending the weaponry to anti-Israeli militants.

January 10, 2002 President Bush warns Iran against harboring al-Qaeda operatives.

January 29, 2002 In his first State of the Union address, President Bush declares Iran to be part of an "axis of evil," along with Iraq and North Korea. Foreign Minister Khatami rejects Bush's speech as "bellicose and insulting"; Rafsanjani hints at oil boycott; Foreign Minister Kharrazi cancels a visit to New York City.

February 11, 2002	Iran commemorates its revolution's anniversary with the largest anti-U.S. protests in years; President Khatami calls on Washington's "immature leaders" to change their stance.
February 13, 2002	The United States and Israel block Iran's application to the WTO.
April 9, 2002	Secretary of State Powell confirms appeals to Tehran to restrain Hezbollah.
May 9, 2002	The U.S. government imposes sanctions on Chinese, Armenian, and Moldovan companies accused of aiding the Iranian nuclear program.
May 10, 2002	U.S. and Iranian diplomats meet in Paris for discussions on the Nagorno-Karabakh dispute.
Late May 2002	Tehran's judiciary bans press discussion of negotiations with the United States; Khatami pledges not to negotiate with Washington.
December 7, 2002	Iran announces fingerprinting policy toward U.S. visitors in retaliation for U.S. immigration restrictions.
December 2002	The United States accuses Iran of seeking to develop a secret nuclear weapons program and publishes satellite images of two nuclear sites under construction at Natanz and Arak.
June 11–13, 2003	Antigovernment protests erupt in Tehran; several thousand young Iranians are arrested; the State Department issues a statement of support for the protesters.
June 19, 2003	The International Atomic Energy Agency (IAEA) board of governors calls on Iran to comply with its Nonproliferation Treaty (NPT) obligations; President Bush announces the world will not permit an Iranian nuclear weapons capability and encourages Iranians to oppose the regime.

August 2003	The IAEA confirms finding weapons-grade uranium at the Iranian nuclear facility in Natanz.
September 12, 2003	The IAEA unanimously approves an October 31 deadline for Iran to prove it is not developing nuclear weapons.
September 25, 2003	IAEA inspectors confirm that highly enriched uranium was found at the Kalaye Electric Company near Tehran.
October 21, 2003	In a deal brokered by three European foreign ministers, Iran agrees to suspend its uranium-enrichment program and sign the Additional Protocol of the NPT.
November 26, 2003	The IAEA board of governors issues a resolution condemning Iran's past concealment of nuclear activities and welcoming new cooperation with Tehran.
December 18, 2003	Iran signs the NPT Additional Protocol, agreeing to enhanced scrutiny of its nuclear programs.
December 2003	Washington sends humanitarian aid to Iran after an earthquake in Bam kills up to 30,000 people; it also relaxes sanctions to facilitate additional U.S. private assistance; U.S. and Iranian officials speak directly to coordinate aid.
March 13, 2004	The IAEA approves a resolution that defers progress in verifying Iranian declarations about its nuclear activities until its June meeting.

APPENDIX B

IRAN AT A GLANCE*

IRAN AT A GLANCE: FACTS AND FIGURES	
Population	68,278,826 (July 2003 est.)
Ethnic groups	Persian: 51% Azeri Turk: 24% Gilaki and Mazandarani: 8% Kurd: 7%; Arab: 3%; Lur: 2%; Baloch: 2%; Turkmen: 2%; other: 1%
Religions	Shia Muslim: 89% Sunni Muslim: 10% Zoroastrian, Jewish, Christian, and Baha'i: 1%
Size of military forces *Source:* International Institute for Strategic Studies, *The Military Balance, 2002/2003*	Army: 325,000 Navy: 18,000 Air Force: 52,000 Revolutionary Guard Navy: 20,000 Revolutionary Guard Marines: 5,000 Revolutionary Guard Ground Forces: 100,000
DEMOGRAPHICS	
Percentage of population under 15 *Source:* Population Division of the Department of Economic and Social Affairs of the United Nations	35.2% (2001)
Percentage of population under 24 *Source:* Population Division of the Department of Economic and Social Affairs of the United Nations Secretariat	59% (2001)
Annual population growth rate *Source:* World Bank 2004 World Development Indicators	2.3% (1980–2004)
Urban population as a percentage of total population *Source: UNDP Human Development Report 2003*	64.7% (2001) 45.8% (1975)

* Unless otherwise noted, the source for all information is the *CIA World Factbook, 2003.*

ECONOMY	
Gross domestic product (GDP)	$458.3 billion (2002 est.)
GDP per capita	$6,800 (2002 est.)
GDP growth rate	7.6% (2002 est.)
Population below poverty line	40% (2002 est.)
Unemployment rate	16.3% (2003 est.)
Inflation rate	15.3% (2002 est.)
Proven oil reserves *Source:* U.S. Energy Information Administration	90 billion barrels; 7% of world total
Proven natural gas reserves *Source:* U.S. Energy Information Administration	812 trillion cubic feet; 15% of world total
Government spending on food subsidies, as percentage of GDP *Source:* IMF	2% (2002 est.)
Size of state sector as a percentage of all industrial enterprises *Source:* IMF	70%

Expenditures as percentage of GDP:
  Military
  Education
Source: UNDP Human Development Report 2003
	4.8% (2001)
	4.4% (1998–2000)

SOCIETY	
Freedom House ratings *(on a scale of 1 to 7, with 1 representing the highest degree of freedom and 7 the lowest level of freedom)* *Source:* Freedom House	Political rights: 6 (out of 7) Civil liberties: 6 (out of 7) Status: Not free (2003)
"Brain drain": number of annual educated émigrés *Source:* IMF	150,000–180,000 ($11 billion in intellectual assets)

School enrollment ratio, females as percentage of males
  Primary school enrollment ratio
  Secondary school enrollment ratio
Source: UNICEF
	97%
	93%
	(1997–2000)

Literacy rate, total population
  Men
  Women
  Youth (ages 15–24)
Source: CIA World Factbook; UNDP
Human Development Report 2003
	79.4%
	85.6%
	73.0%
	94.2%
	
	(2003 est.)

Total enrollment in public universities and colleges *Source:* IMF	1,566,000
University acceptances by gender *Source:* Statistical Centre of Iran Women as percentage of total labor force *Source: World Bank GenderStats*	Male: 48%; Female 52% 27% (2000)
Women in government at ministerial level (as percentage of total) *Source: UNDP Human Development* *Report 2003*	9.4% (2000)
Internet users (per 1,000) *Source: UNDP Human Development* *Report 2003*	15.3 (2001)
Percentage of Iranians who support relations with the United States, according to 2002 internal poll *Source:* Radio Free Europe/Radio Liberty	74%
Percentage of Iranians who participate in weekly or more frequent religious services, according to 2000–2001 survey *Source:* National Science Foundation	12%
Number of nongovernmental organizations *Source:* Radio Free Europe/Radio Liberty	More than 8,000

IRANIAN STATE INSTITUTIONS AND POLITICAL ACTORS

THE IRANIAN STATE: INSTITUTIONS OF GOVERNANCE	

Iran's Religious Governance *(velayat-e faqih)*
 	
Head:
Ayatollah Ali Khamenei (since 1989)
	Iran's constitution empowers the clergy to select the best qualified to serve as ruling jurist *(vali-ye faqih)* or Leader *(rahbar)*. His powers include:
	  • Approval/dismissal of the president
	  • Supervision over the general policies of the government
	  • Commander-in-chief of the armed forces; power to declare war
	  • Appointment of judiciary and control over radio and television broadcasting and a host of other public institutions
	    Other spheres of influence include parastatal economic organizations, Friday prayer leader network, and representatives of the office of the Leader deployed throughout the country and throughout the bureaucracy.
	    In 1989, constitutional revisions abolished the requirement that the Leader be recognized by his clerical peers as a *marja*, or recognized source of emulation, and removed stipulations for a leadership council.
	    Since the revolution, the powers of the Leader have progressively expanded. In 1988, his mandate was made absolute and elevated to the highest order of divine commandment, and the 1989 constitutional revisions explicitly gave him the position of "absolute general trusteeship" over the government.
	    Since 1989, the office of the Leader has grown considerably in size, scope, and authority. Khamenei typically aligns himself with his conservative base but has proved capable of compromise with reformers. His absolute authority is somewhat constrained as a result of his relatively modest rank in the clerical hierarchy.

The Presidency	Due to postrevolutionary jockeying for power, the presidency of the Islamic Republic was intended to be administratively impotent. Originally, the president's role was a formality, and a prime minister formulated and implemented policy. In 1989, Khomeini's death prompted a modest reconfiguration of the system, eliminating the office of the prime minister and converting the presidency to the nominal head of government. Presidential elections are held every four years, and the post is subject to a constitutional two-term limit. The presidency remains explicitly subordinated to the Leader and wields relatively limited material authority through its oversight of the various cabinet ministries. The president sits on powerful governmental bodies,

	but his power is contingent upon informal relationships with other power brokers. In 2002, Khatami introduced two bills for parliamentary consideration that would have considerably strengthened the constitutional authority of the president. The Guardian Council twice rejected these bills, and there is little prospect of their revival or implementation.
Council of Guardians (*Shura-ye Negahban*) *Head:* Ayatollah Ahmad Jannati	This body of twelve judges is comprised of six religious jurists and six laypeople. It is empowered to review all legislation to check its conformity with both Islam and Iran's constitution, and is also given responsibility for supervising elections. Iran's constitution empowers the six clerics on the council with relatively wide jurisdiction. The Supreme Leader plays a major role in the selection and oversight of the Council of Guardians. In the 1980s, the council regularly clashed with parliament over ideology, blocking two important efforts of the postrevolutionary government—land reform and nationalization of foreign trade—on the basis of a traditionalist interpretation of Islamic law. Conflicts with parliament during the 1980s led to the adoption of a new principle for decision-making—*maslehat*, or expediency—that formally elevated Iranian nationalist interests above all other considerations, including the constraints of Islamic law. Since 1992, the council has taken vast latitude to determine the relative freedom of elections by appropriating the authority to determine the eligibility of candidates for elected office.
Islamic Consultative Assembly (*Majlis-e Shura-ye Islami*)	The Iranian parliament dates back to the 1905–11 Constitutional Revolution. Today its powers include: • Oversight of the executive branch (via approval/impeachment of cabinet ministers) • Ratification of international agreements • Responsibility for economic policymaking through drafting the annual government budget and approving the long-term planning process Constraints on the Majlis are considerable. All legislation must be reviewed and approved by the Council of Guardians.
Assembly of Experts (*Majlis-e Khobregan*) *Head:* Ayatollah Ali Meshkini	The Assembly of Experts was established in 1979 as an elite constitutional assembly and disbanded soon after the constitution was approved. A new Assembly of Experts was convened in 1982 over concerns about succession, with the primary responsibility for selection of the Supreme Leader. It is comprised of eighty-six religious scholars who are elected in national balloting to serve eight-year terms. A key requirement for candidates is religious learning, but members need not be clerics (at least in theory). However, candidates are stringently vetted to ensure their lockstep support for the status quo. Because its responsibilities are few and highly episodic, the assembly has little role in Iran's day-to-day politics.

Expediency Council *(Majma-ye Tashkhis-e Maslahat-e Nezam* or Council for Assessing the Interests of the System) *Head:* Former president Hashemi Rafsanjani	Due to persistent conflicts between the parliament and the Council of Guardians, Ayatollah Khomeini ruled in 1988 that the *interests of state* ranked above "all ordinances that were derived or directly commanded by Allah." The Expediency Council was established to institutionalize this principle. Its powers include: ● Mediating between parliament and the Council of Guardians on disputed legislation ● Advising the Leader on broad policies of the state The Expediency Council was expanded in 1997, in preparation for its assumption by then president Hashemi Rafsanjani. Members serve five-year terms. Includes heads of the three branches of government, six clerics on the Guardian Council, relevant cabinet ministers, and others appointed by the Supreme Leader. Decision-making remains shrouded and secretive.

IRANIAN POLITICAL ACTORS

1.) Hard-liners and ultraconservatives

Agenda: Represent the doctrinaire extremist fringe of the conservative camp. Committed to imposing stringent cultural and political restrictions on society in order to achieve their vision of Islamic government and, most importantly, retain their hold on power. Traditionalist Islamic stance on the economy: e.g., antipathy toward government intervention in the market and reliance on Islamic values to address socioeconomic needs. Worldview envisions Iran as the leader of the Islamic world and equates Iranian interests with Islamic interests.

Parties and Organizations:

- Society of Combatant Clerics (*Jame-ye Rouhaniyat-e Mobarez*)

- Society of the Qom Seminary Teachers (*Jame-ye Modareseen-e Hoze-ye Elmiyehh-ye Qom*)

- Devotees of the Party of God (*Ansar-e Hezbollah*)

- Hojjatiyeh Society (*Anjoman-e Hojjatiyeh*)

- Islamic Coalition Society (*Jameyat-e Motalefe-ye Eslami*)

Leading Figures:

- Ayatollah Mohammad Yazdi: Former head of the judiciary and member of the Council of Guardians

- Ayatollah Ali Meshkini: Head of the Assembly of Experts

- Habibollah Asgarowladi: Secretary general of Motalefe and former commerce minister and MP in 4th Majlis; involved with leadership of the Foundation of the Oppressed and the Imam Khomeini Relief Foundation

- Alinaghi Khamoushi: Former deputy commerce minister and current head of the Chamber of Commerce and Industry

2.) Moderates and/or "pragmatic" conservatives
Agenda: Favor political moderation, free markets, and cultural tolerance within limits. Prioritize national interests over ideology and economic development above all other issues. Sometimes referred to as the "modern right wing." Rhetoric and policies advocated tend to be centered on socioeconomic development. Downplay religious ideology in favor of republican and pro-market positions. Tend to swing to the right (traditional conservatives) and to the left (reformists) to maximize influence.

Parties and Organizations:

- Servants of Construction (*Hezb-e Kargozaran-e Sazandegi*)

- Islamic Iran Developers' Council (*Etelaf-e Abadgaran-e Iran-e Eslami*)

- Development and Moderation Party (*Hezb-e Etedal va Tose'e*)

Leading Figures:

- Hojjatoleslam Akbar Hashemi Rafsanjani: Former president

- Hojjatoleslam Hassan Rouhani: Secretary of the National Security Council and former deputy speaker of parliament

- Ahmad Tavakoli: Former labor minister and leading vote-getter in 2004 parliamentary elections

3.) Mainstream reformists
Agenda: Encompasses a broad ideological spectrum and a multiplicity of organizations and advocates. Generally, mainstream reformists favor mass political participation, sociocultural tolerance and liberalization, and international engagement. Until recently, they were united in a commitment to achieve these objectives within the limitations of the current constitution. On the economy, some reformist organizations and leaders remain heavily imprinted with the ideological baggage of revolutionary populism and support redistributive policies and a strong state role. Today, however, most recognize the state's limitations in improving Iran's economic predicament.

Parties and Organizations:

- Association of Combatant Clerics (*Majma-ye Rouhaniyun-e Mobarez*)

- Islamic Iran Participation Front (*Jebhe-ye Mosharekat-e Iran-e Eslami*)

- Mojahideen of the Islamic Revolution (*Sazeman-e Mojahideen-e Enqelab-e Eslami*)

- Islamic Iran Solidarity Party (*Hezb-e Hambastegi-e Iran-e Islami*)

- Islamic Labor Party (*Hezb-e Islami Kar*)

Leading Figures:

- Hojjatoleslam Mohammad Khatami: President

- Hojjatoleslam Ali Akbar Mohtashamipour: Former ambassador to Syria; former minister of intelligence; considered the founder of Lebanese Hezbollah

- Mohammad Reza Khatami: Member and deputy speaker of the 6th Majlis; former publisher of IIPF's now-banned newspaper *Mosharekat* ("Participation"); former deputy minister of health; former professor, Tehran University medical school; married to granddaughter of Ayatollah Khomeini

- Saeed Hajarian: Former deputy minister of intelligence; close political adviser to President Khatami; elected member of the Tehran City Council until 2000 assassination attempt nearly cost him his life; editor of the now-banned daily *Sobh-e Emrooz*

- Behzad Nabavi: Former minister of heavy industry; former vice speaker of the 6th Majlis; served as Iran's lead negotiator during negotiations with the United States over hostage crisis; recently targeted in corruption scandal involving semiprivate oil company

- Mohsen Mirdamadi: Member of the 6th Majlis and chairman of the Majlis National Security and Foreign Affairs Committee; former director of IIPF's now-banned newspaper *Norouz* ("New Year")

4.) Liberal opposition forces
Agenda: Despite government repression, a small corps of individuals and organizations have remained active opponents of the government from within Iran. Chief among these groups is the Freedom Movement, which played a leading role in the revolution and its early aftermath. Its leader, Mehdi Bazargan, resigned as head of the provisional government in 1979 to protest the seizure of the U.S. embassy. The group survived as a unique and grudgingly tolerated critic of the Islamic regime but was officially banned as of July 2002. Its members remain vocal detractors of Iran's system of religious governance through their writings and through other political organizations.

Parties and Organizations:

- Freedom Movement of Iran (*Nezhat-e Azadi-ye Iran*)

- Religious-Nationalist Alliance (*Nirooha-ye Melli Mazhabi*)

Leading Figures:

- Dr. Ibrahim Yazdi: Former foreign minister in the provisional government; indicted while on an extended stay in the United States for cancer treatment and returned to Iran in April 2002 to face prosecution

- Ezzatollah Sahabi: Son of one of the founding members of the Freedom Movement and active in the liberal opposition during the 1960s

5) Student organizations

   Agenda: The Islamic government established student organizations as part of the cultural revolution that was promulgated during the 1980s. Today, these organizations have evolved to reflect the views of their membership, rather than inculcating regime loyalty, and are strident opponents of the Islamic regime. Many student leaders split early on from the mainstream reform movement in pressing for a more progressive agenda and a more aggressive effort to confront conservatives.

Parties and Organizations:

- Office for Consolidation of Unity (*Daftar-e Takhim-e Vahdat*)

- Union of Islamic Students (*Ettehadi-ye Eslami-ye Daneshjuyan*)

Leading Figures:

- Ali Afshari: Sentenced for his participation in an April 2000 conference in Berlin and subsequently prosecuted for accusing the Revolutionary Guards of torturing him to gain a false confession

- Ahmad Batebi: Serving a fifteen-year jail sentence for his role in the July 1999 student protests; Batebi was made famous in a photo on the cover of *The Economist* magazine

6) Dissident clerics

- Grand Ayatollah Hossein Ali Montazeri: Designated Ayatollah Khomeini's heir apparent in 1985, Montazeri was stripped of this post and shunned from active political life in 1989, after protesting a regime crackdown; spent years under house arrest until his release last year; Montazeri continues to inspire an active circle of adherents, who favor his emphasis on the democratic features of Iran's Islamic system and who echo his frequent searing critiques of the regime

- Ayatollah Jalaloddin Taheri: Former Friday prayer leader in Isfahan who resigned his position in July 2002 with a widely published appeal against the corruption and violence that had infected the senior ranks of the Islamic Republic; he also called for an end to Montazeri's house arrest

- Grand Ayatollah Yusef Sanei: Once a student of Ayatollah Khomeini, Sanei has been one of the most senior and outspoken proponents of a liberal interpretation of Islam; he is a member of the Council of Guardians and remains a defender of Montazeri.

- Hojjatoleslam Mohsen Kadivar: Professor of philosophy at Tarbiat Modares University who was arrested in February 1999 for his scathing critique of the absolutist implementation of Islamic government; head of Society in Defense of Press Freedom; served eighteen months in prison

- Hojjatoleslam Hassan Yousefi Eshkevari: Arrested and sentenced to death in connection with his participation at an April 2000 conference in Berlin; he was released in August 2002 but subsequently rearrested and sentenced to seven years' imprisonment

7) Dissident intellectuals and journalists

- Abbas Abdi: Former student leader (and central figure in seizure of U.S. hostages in 1979) turned liberal journalist; currently serving a four-year jail term for his role in conducting an October 2002 opinion poll that demonstrated widespread popular support for relations with the United States

- Hashem Aghajari: Professor at Tarbiat Modarres University convicted for apostasy after a speech rejecting the notion of absolute clerical authority; his death sentence set off protests across the country and, after much high-level maneuvering, was revoked; Aghajari is currently in jail pending retrial

- Emadeddin Baqi: Writer/journalist who has criticized the Islamic Republic from the standpoint of his seminary education; imprisoned in 2000 for "insulting Islam" and freed after serving nearly three years; Baqi was summoned again and convicted of anti-regime activities in December 2003

- Akbar Ganji: Revolutionary bureaucrat turned writer who helped expose official complicity in the "serial murders" of dissidents; prior to the 2000 parliamentary elections he accused former President Hashemi Rafsanjani of masterminding the violence as well as prolonging the war with Iraq; arrested for participation in April 2000 conference in Berlin and sentenced to ten years in jail

- Mohsen Sazegara: Prominent dissident journalist who was one of the early critics of the timidity of President Khatami and the reformists generally; arrested in connection with June 2003 student protests and released on health concerns after a hunger strike; his conviction was recently upheld

- Mashallah Shamsolvaezin: Edited a string of daring reformist newspapers, reopening under a new name within days of judicial closures of each publication; jailed in 2000 for criticism of the Iranian policy of capital punishment and released after seventeen months in prison, he was recently summoned again by the judiciary for his articles on the parliamentary elections crisis

- Abdolkarim Soroush: Once a leading agent of Iran's postrevolutionary cultural revolution, Soroush has been dubbed the "Iranian Martin Luther" for his writings on Islamic interpretation, which reject the notion of religion as ideology; he has argued that Islam and democracy are fully compatible; Soroush was targeted in the mid-1990s by hard-line thugs

8) External opposition forces

Mojahideen-e Khalq Organization
The MKO is a left-wing group, established in the 1960s, that initially supported the Islamic Republic and had a long history of working with clerical groups and leaders who opposed the shah. After the revolution, the MKO and clerics clashed violently, and Mojahideen leaders fled to conduct a resistance in exile. Their collaboration with Saddam Hussein throughout the Iran-Iraq War means that the group retains little if any viability as an alternative political movement among Iranians. The MKO and its political arm, the National Council of Resistance, were added to the U.S. State Department's list of foreign terrorist organizations in 1997. Four thousand MKO members in Iraq have been officially "detained" in their camps by U.S. occupying forces, although how their situation will be ultimately handled remains uncertain.

Reza Pahlavi
The son of the late shah has become more politically active in recent years, and he has been embraced by some U.S. policymakers and by a sizable minority of Iranian-Americans as a potential "cata-

lyst" for democratic change. Nostalgia for what are now considered the halcyon days of the shah extends to the Islamic Republic, but some there question Pahlavi's ambitions and consider him too long removed from the country to offer any prospect of leadership.

Exiled student dissidents

Since the violent demonstrations of July 1999 and June 2003, some students have fled and mobilized to oppose the regime in exile. Aryo Pirouznia and his group, the Student Committee for Coordination of Democracy in Iran, are frequently quoted—but it is unclear to what extent they remain networked to Iran's student leadership.

Other opposition organizations

Many small political organizations have emerged in recent years to promote political change in Iran, some as outgrowths of liberal opposition movements from the prerevolutionary period. Few appear able to sustain significant membership or activities, either abroad or in Iran, despite laudable agendas.

Satellite television

Without powerful expatriate organizations, the most effective link among Iranians abroad and those still in the country is the medium of satellite television. Programs actively encourage anti-regime activities. They are popular in the United States and in Iran, but many dissidents within the country deride their agitation as emanating from "armchair revolutionaries."